B

Athens

Victoria Kyriakopoulos

Best of Athens
2nd edition – March 2004
First published – May 2002

Published by Lonely Planet Publications Pty Ltd
ABN 36 005 607 983

Australia	Head Office, Locked Bag 1, Footscray, Vic 3011
	☎ 03 8379 8000 fax 03 8379 8111
	🖳 talk2us@lonelyplanet.com.au
USA	150 Linden St, Oakland, CA 94607
	☎ 510 893 8555 toll free 800 275 8555
	fax 510 893 8572
	🖳 info@lonelyplanet.com
UK	72–82 Rosebery Avenue, London EC1R 4RW
	☎ 020 7841 9000 fax 020 7841 9001
	🖳 go@lonelyplanet.co.uk
France	1 rue du Dahomey, 75011 Paris
	☎ 01 55 25 33 00 fax 01 55 25 33 01
	🖳 bip@lonelyplanet.fr
	🖳 www.lonelyplanet.fr

This title was commissioned in Lonely Planet's London office and produced by: **Commissioning Editor** Michala Green **Coordinating Editor** Imogen Bannister **Coordinating Cartographer** Daniel Fennessy **Layout Designer** Yvonne Bischofberger **Editor** Jocelyn Harewood **Proofer** Helen Yeates **Indexer** Darren O'Connell **Cartographer** Natasha Velleley **Managing Cartographer** Mark Griffiths **Cover Designer** Gerilyn Attebery **Project Manager** Charles Rawlings-Way **Series Designer** Gerilyn Attebery **Mapping Development** Paul Piaia **Regional Publishing Manager** Katrina Browning **Thanks to** Adriana Mammarella, Fiona Siseman, Hunor Csutoros, Jacqui Saunders, Michelle Lewis, Piotr Czajkowski, Sally Darmody & Steven Cann

© Lonely Planet Publications Pty Ltd 2004.

All rights reserved.

Photographs by Lonely Planet Images © (2004) and Anders Blomqvist except for the following as listed: p12, p13, p17 p18, p21, p22, p24, p27, p28, p37, p39, p45, p59, p61, p65, p67 Neil Setchfield; p18 John Borthwick; p23, p47 George Tsafos; p47, p48, p49 John Elk III; p50 Kim Wildman; p55 Brenda Turnnidge and p70 Alan Benson. **Cover photograph** Temple of Olympian Zeus, Chad Ehlers/Photolibrary.com. All images are copyright of the photographers unless otherwise indicated. Many of the images in this guide are available for licensing from Lonely Planet Images 🖳 www.lonelyplanetimages.com.

ISBN 1 74059 506 8

Printed through Colorcraft Ltd, Hong Kong.
Printed in China

Lonely Planet and the Lonely Planet logo are trademarks of Lonely Planet and are registered in the US Patent and Trademark Office and in other countries.

Lonely Planet does not allow its name or logo to be appropriated by commercial establishments, such as retailers, restaurants or hotels. Please let us know of any misuses: 🖳 www.lonelyplanet.com/ip

HOW TO USE THIS BOOK

Colour-Coding & Maps

Each chapter has a colour code along the banner at the top of the page which is also used for text and symbols on maps (eg, all venues reviewed in the Highlights chapter are orange on the maps). The fold-out maps inside the front and back covers are numbered from 1 to 9. All sights and venues in the text have map references; eg, (9, C3) means Map 9, grid reference C3. See p128 for map symbols.

Prices

Multiple prices listed with reviews (eg €10/5) usually indicate adult/concession admission to a venue. Concession prices can include senior, student, member or coupon discounts. Meal cost and room rate categories are listed at the start of the Eating and Sleeping chapters, respectively.

Text Symbols

☎ telephone
⊠ address
🖳 email/website address
€ admission
☺ opening hours
ⓘ information
Ⓜ metro
🚌 bus
🚕 taxi/car
⚓ ferry
🚊 tram/trolleybus
♿ wheelchair access
⊠ on site/nearby eatery
♿ child-friendly venue

Contents

From the Publisher

AUTHOR

Victoria Kyriakopoulos

A regular visitor to Athens since 1988, Victoria moved to the Greek capital in 2000, and has watched the city undergo a massive upheaval as it prepares for the Olympics. Like most Athenians, she has learnt to accept and manoeuvre around the city's quirky and chaotic nature, helped along by a good sense of humour, healthy cynicism, increased assertiveness, the occasional frustrated outburst – and regular escapes to the mainland, islands or out of the country altogether.

While she concedes that Athens can be a love-it or hate-it place, she is keen to ensure visitors are equipped to discover its often hidden charms and decide for themselves.

Victoria wrote the first edition of Lonely Planet's *Athens Condensed* and was editor of *Odyssey* magazine until May 2003. She is currently a freelance writer for various Australian publications, including the *Age* newspaper, and an occasional stringer for ABC radio. In her home town of Melbourne, she had various career incarnations, including stints as a staff writer with the *Bulletin*, columnist for the *Age*, government press secretary and reporter on the *Melbourne Herald*.

Thanks to Maria Zygourakis, Chris Anastassiades, Mary Retiniotis, Vicky Valanos, Antonis Bekiaris and Eleni Bertes.

PHOTOGRAPHER

Anders Blomqvist

Originally from Sweden, but now considering himself a citizen of Planet Earth, Anders Blomqvist has travelled the world for over 25 years in pursuit of a good time and great photos. He has worked on a luxury liner, and for over 10 years as a trekking and rafting guide in Nepal, Tibet, Norway and Australia.

He now divides his time between a small coastal village in southern Sweden, and Asia or the Middle East.

SEND US YOUR FEEDBACK

We love to hear from travellers – your comments keep us on our toes and help make our books better. Our well-travelled team reads every word on what you loved or loathed about this book. Although we cannot reply individually to postal submissions, we always guarantee that your feedback goes straight to the appropriate authors, in time for the next edition – and the most useful submissions are rewarded with a free book. To send us your updates – and find out about LP events, newsletters and travel news – visit our award-winning website 🖳 www.lonelyplanet.com.

Note: We may edit, reproduce and incorporate your comments in Lonely Planet products such as guidebooks, websites and digital products, so let us know if you don't want your comments reproduced or your name acknowledged. For a copy of our privacy policy visit 🖳 www.lonelyplanet.com/privacy.

Introducing Athens

Modern Athens was always going to have it tough living up to its past glory. Whatever it did, the awe-inspiring Acropolis stood above the city, a reminder of its revered historic achievements in the arts, philosophy, architecture and politics.

While the history and ancient monuments fascinated visitors, the concrete sprawl that lay beyond failed to inspire. Few fell in love with Athens at first sight.

But, with the 2004 Olympics as a catalyst, much-maligned Athens has spent the past decade transforming itself into a modern, efficient European capital. When Athens presents its new face to the world, it may well prove a pleasant surprise, though the capital will never overcome the damage done during the postwar building boom.

The city's renaissance includes a new airport, a modern metro system, new highways, more open, green space, beautification of the historic centre and transformation of run-down areas into vibrant neighbourhoods. Since joining the euro brigade, it has also become a far more expensive city.

But much of Athens' appeal has always lain beyond the façade, in its quirky pulse and energy and rather anarchistic nature. The city's chaos and contradictions can be as seductive as they are frustrating, its communal angst counterbalanced by a zest for the good life.

The pace can be fast (the public service aside) but people still take time out for endless coffees. Pink evening skies over the Acropolis and city walks through the historic centre never fail to impress. The lively restaurants and bars, almost year-round sunshine and the seasonal dynamics of Athenian life make for a vibrant city.

Athens is alive long after the rest of Europe has gone to bed – and there's certainly something oddly life-affirming about 3am traffic.

A hard act to follow: a view of the Acropolis and Parthenon from Filopappos Hill

Neighbourhoods

Sightseeing in Athens involves lots of walking, mostly around the centre and historic areas of Plaka and Monastiraki, where the majority of museums and major sights are concentrated.

Beyond the usual tourist route, however, there are many interesting neighbourhoods to explore, each with its unique character. Venturing

away from the centre can be very rewarding and will certainly give you a better glimpse of the spectrum of modern Athenian life.

Overrun by tourists in summer, the historic neighbourhoods under the Acropolis nonetheless retain their charm. Locals still come to **Plaka's** tavernas and cafés, making it a lively quarter year-round. While many of the traditional stores on the main streets have been replaced by souvenir and jewellery

Time for refuelling at a Plaka eatery

stores, you can still wander off the tourist strip and get a glimpse of the old neighbourhood. **Monastiraki** is a little grungier, but arguably more interesting to walk around, with its curious mix of stores, the flea market and quirky corners such as Plateia Avyssinias.

Many people love the earthiness of **Exarhia**, posh Kolonaki's bohemian neighbour. Although parts have been gentrified, it's still popular with students and left-wing intellectuals due to its historic association with radical politics and the student movements of the junta era (it's near the university). Exarhia is also home to many cheap tavernas, good cafés, alternative book, music and clothing stores, *rebetika* clubs and small live-music venues.

The revival of the former semi-industrial area **Gazi** started with the innovative transformation of the historic gasworks into an impressive cultural centre (p39). Gazi has become a happening place. Many derelict buildings

Indulge in some retail therapy at the Monastiraki Flea Market

have been restored and turned into trendy restaurants and bars, and big warehouses turned into nightclubs – and the trend is spreading to nearby **Rouf**.

The new tram line along the coast to **Glyfada** is sure to give the former resort town a huge boost, as will the major face-lift of surrounding suburbs and the former airport site, which is to be a massive metropolitan park post-Olympics. Summer nightlife traditionally moves to the waterfront and Glyfada has many fine restaurants and excellent shopping.

Leafy **Kifissia** was once a cool northern retreat, where rich Athenians had their villas. It still is, although it is now more of a classy upmarket suburb with its own elegant character and great bars, restaurants and shopping. The mansions and tree-lined streets and gardens are a far cry from the urban centre – another world only 12km north of Athens.

Historically an elite residential neighbourhood, **Kolonaki** is the most classy – and flashy – part of central Athens. The chic boutiques, fine restaurants and galleries are concentrated around and off the main square, where the outdoor cafés are constantly full. It certainly has a buzz, but it can be overrun by fashion victims (though this is part of the fun). Things get more dignified away from the square up towards **Lykavittos Hill** and around **Dexameni**.

> **Off the Beaten Track**
> If you want to get away from the tourist bustle, you can't go wrong with a drive up to the **Kaisariani monastery** (p28). Closer to town, the ancient cemetery of Athens at **Keramikos** (p26) is one of the more green, peaceful and less-frequented archaeological sites. Alternatively, you venture outside Athens to the **Koutouki Cave** (p42) and **Vorres Museum** (p42).

A quiet sanctuary, Kaisariani monastery

The Soho of Athens has a deceptively seedy façade, but **Psiri's** narrow streets are bustling at night with people heading to a plethora of restaurants and bars in this newly fashionable district. Renowned for its live music, particularly a tradition of merry late Sunday afternoons, Psiri is lively long after Plaka has shut down. Several hip galleries have opened in disused warehouses, but it retains an offbeat mix of old stores, bakeries and workshops.

Beyond its function as the main port of Athens, **Piraeus** is a bustling, chaotic city in its own right. Most tourists go there to catch a ferry, and in truth there aren't many sights, although the Archaeological Museum (p32) is excellent. While there are some fine eateries scattered through Piraeus town and the port, the area's highlight is the picturesque Mikrolimano harbour, lined with cafés, bars and restaurants.

Itineraries

Ancient Athens was tiny compared to the sprawling metropolis of today. This makes it easy for visitors to see the historic centre, major landmarks and attractions; the rest of the city is a little more complex.

There are many gems to be discovered just by walking around the city. As most of the important archaeological sites and museums are within walking distance of the centre (and each other), seeing the city on foot is the best option.

If you are visiting in summer, it is best to see the archaeological sites early in the morning and spend the hottest part of the day at a museum. Many sites and state-run museums close by 2pm – another reason to go early. On the other hand, heading to the Acropolis a little later might mean you avoid the tour groups. Make sure you wear rubber-soled shoes as the ancient marble surfaces can be very slippery and uneven.

Lowlights

Things that can stress you out in Athens:

- Traffic, noise and Athens' drivers
- Pavements that can be uneven, potholed and treacherous
- Having to yell to hail a speeding taxi in peak hour
- The small but nasty percentage of rip-off taxi drivers
- The early closing hours of many sights
- Strikes by taxis and archaeological site employees
- Astronomical post-euro prices, especially for coffee and drinks

DAY ONE

Head to the **Acropolis** (p9), Athens' crowning jewel, and the **Ancient Agora** (p15), then amble through **Plaka** and **Anafiotika** (p13). Walk through the **Roman Agora** (p20) and the **Tower of the Winds** before browsing the **Monastiraki Flea Market** (p54). Explore the significant collection of the **National Archaeological Museum** (p12). In the evening, see the changing of the guards at Syntagma, before dining under the Acropolis in Plaka (p75) or Thisio (p69). Head to a bar or catch some live Greek music in Psiri (p87).

DAY TWO

Go to the **Museum of Cycladic and Ancient Greek Art** (p19) and the **Benaki Museum** (p16) where you can lunch on the rooftop overlooking the **National Gardens** (p38). Visit the **Byzantine and Christian Museum** (p23) then wander through Kolonaki's boutiques (p55) and cafés (p81). Catch an evening show at the **Theatre of Herodes Atticus** (p24) or take the funicular railway up **Lykavittos Hill** (p17) for a panoramic view of Athens.

DAY THREE

Visit the **National Art Gallery** (p21), stroll through the **National Gardens** (p38) and stop for a coffee at **Aigli** (p78), then walk over to the **Panathenaic Stadium** (p18) and the **Temple of Olympian Zeus** (p25). Head into Plaka or Ermou for some shopping (p53). Go to Piraeus' Mikrolimano port for a seafood dinner (p79) by the water and a drink at a swish bar (p90).

Highlights

ACROPOLIS (9, C3)

Even when you live in Athens, the sight of the Acropolis can still make your heart skip a beat. Time, war, pilfering, earthquakes and pollution have taken their toll on the sacred hill and its crowning glory, the Parthenon (p11) – yet it stands defiant and dignified over Athens and remains one of the most important ancient sites in the Western world.

Many of the Acropolis' monuments have, unfortunately, been stripped or destroyed over the years or put into museums, so there are replicas in place. A 20-year restoration project is attempting to redress deterioration from age, industrial pollution, traffic fumes and previous restorations. The site is now World Heritage listed.

First inhabited in Neolithic times, it served as a fortress, a place of cult worship, and archaeologists believe there was a Mycenaean palace on the peak. Many temples were built on Acropolis (High City) paying homage to the goddess Athena.

After the buildings were destroyed by the Persians in 480 BC, Pericles began his ambitious build-

INFORMATION
- ☎ 210 321 0219
- 🖳 www.culture.gr
- ✉ Acropolis (enter from Dionysiou Areopagitou or Theorias)
- € €12 (valid four days & includes entrance to Roman & Ancient Agoras, Keramikos, Temple of Olympian Zeus & Dionysos Theatre)
- 🕗 8am-7pm (8am-5pm Nov-Mar)
- ⓘ Opens once a year for full moon, see p20
- Ⓜ Akropoli

ing programme, which transformed the Acropolis into a magnificent city of temples. In subsequent years, it served as the military stronghold for successive occupiers and the buildings were converted into Christian churches, mosques and other structures (including a belltower on the Parthenon later converted to a minaret). All Frankish and Turkish structures were removed after independence.

DON'T MISS
- the 6th-century *kora* (maiden) statues in room 4 of the museum
- superb views from the platform
- Nike adjusting her sandal in room 8
- the *moschoforos* (calf-bearer) with his gift to Athena

In 1687, the Venetians attacked the ruling Turks and opened fire on the Acropolis causing a massive explosion (the Ottomans stored gunpowder in the Parthenon) that severely damaged the buildings.

Entry is through the **Beulé Gate and Monument**, built in the 3rd century AD in response to successive invasions.

Beyond it is the **Propylaia**, built 437–432 BC, which formed the monumental entrance to the Acropolis. With a central hall and two wings, it had five gates leading to the city above. The western portico has six imposing double-columns (Doric on the outside and Ionic inside) and the ceiling was painted dark blue with gold stars. The northern wing was used as a picture gallery, with couches for officials. One of the Propylaia's gates led to the **Panathenaic Way**, the route taken by the Panathenaic procession at the end of the festival dedicated to Athena, cutting through the middle of the Acropolis. It began at Keramikos and ended at the Erechtheion.

The bits of the Parthenon Lord Elgin couldn't fit in his suitcase

The **Temple of Athena Nike**, originally built by Callicrates (c 420 BC) on the southwestern edge, has undergone several reconstructions. The most recent saw the elegant, small temple removed altogether in late 2002 (it was to be re-erected by 2004). Only fragments remain of the frieze that ran around the temple, which depicted victory scenes from battles *(nikae)*. Some are in the museum on site, others in the British Museum. A statue of Athena that once graced the temple was most likely destroyed by the Persians.

The **Erechtheion** was built on the site's most sacred spot – where, in a contest for the city, Poseidon struck the ground with his trident producing a spring of water and Athena in turn produced the olive tree (she won).

Named after Erichthonius, the mythical king of Athens, the temple was completed in 420 BC and housed the cults of Athena, Poseidon and Erichthonius. The six maidens that support the portico instead of columns are the famous Caryatids, modelled on the women from Karyai. The ones you see are plaster casts. The originals (except for one taken by Lord Elgin) are in the Acropolis Museum. Despite being overshadowed by the Parthenon, the Erechtheion held greater ritual significance and was the final destination for the Panatheniac procession.

Apart from the workshops where archaeologists painstakingly restore and catalogue the site's fragments, the only other new building on the hill is the **Acropolis Museum**, which houses many sculptures and reliefs from the site. The exhibits are in chronological order, from temples predating the Parthenon.

Going Underground

Even if you don't plan to take a train, a visit to one of Athens' splendid metro stations is a must. Construction of Athens' underground rail network turned into Greece's biggest archaeological dig. Graves, foundations of ancient structures, ancient wells and thousands of artefacts were found in the process, causing major delays. Many finds are exhibited in the metro stations, with excellent displays at Akropoli and Evangelismos. Syntagma station, all gleaming marble and spotless, is a veritable museum displaying finds uncovered during excavations.

Parthenon   (9, C3)

The symbol of the glory of ancient Greece, the Parthenon (Virgin's Chamber) stands on the highest point of the Acropolis. It is the largest Doric temple ever completed in Greece and the only one built entirely of Pentelic marble (apart from its wooden roof). The Parthenon is relatively well preserved, but the current structure also contains fragments of many earlier buildings.

Built on the site of at least four earlier temples dedicated to the goddess (and patron of Rome) Athena, it was the centrepiece of Pericles' Acropolis, finished in time for the Great Panathenaic Festival of 438 BC. As well as housing the great statue of Athena, by Pheidias, the Parthenon served as the treasury for the Delian League.

The temple had eight fluted Doric columns at either end and 17 on each side ingeniously curved to create an optical illusion of a harmonious, perfect form. Brightly coloured and gilded sculptured friezes that ran all the way around (159.5m long) depicted the various battles of the times and the Panathenaic procession. Most of the friezes were damaged in the

1687 explosion, but the greatest existing sections (more than 75m) are the controversial marbles in the British Museum.

Reserved strictly for privileged initiates, the holy *cella* (inner room) contained the colossal 432-BC statue of Athena Parthenos, covered entirely in gold and ivory, which was considered one of the great wonders of the ancient world. The tyrant Lachares is said to have stripped the gold from the awesome 10m-high statue to pay his troops.

Poseidon wonders how to tell Apollo that his hand has gone missing, Acropolis Museum

Lost your Marbles?

The controversial new Acropolis Museum, being built at the southern foot of the Acropolis, has a massive gallery intended for the Parthenon Marbles, built in the hope that international pressure would shame the British Museum into returning them by 2004 – although this is looking highly unlikely.

The marbles were prised off the Parthenon in 1801 by the British Ambassador in Constantinople, Lord Elgin, who sold them to the museum, which in turn scrubbed them in the false belief that they should be white, when in fact they were colourfully painted.

The building designed by acclaimed New York architect Bernard Tschumi will nonetheless eventually provide a stunning showcase for the Acropolis Museum's collection and many other precious finds. It was to open some wings, including the Parthenon gallery, in mid-2004.

NATIONAL ARCHAEOLOGICAL MUSEUM (7, D2)

The museum housing the world's largest and finest collection of Greek antiquities is being refurbished and transformed into a modern facility, befitting the guardian of such a priceless collection. It closed in October 2002 for a complete refurbishment and was to open in time for the 2004 Olympics.

INFORMATION

- ☎ 210 821 7717
- 🖳 www.culture.gr
- ✉ 28 Oktovriou-Patission 44, Athens
- € €6
- 🕑 8am-7pm (8am-5pm Nov-Mar)
- Ⓜ Viktoria
- ⓘ To reopen in June 2004
- ♿ good (lower floors)

Built in the late 1800s, the dated museum, complete with some faded handwritten labels, was in dire need of upgrading. The top floor had been closed since the 1999 earthquake, which sent many of its ancient pots tumbling. Much of the museum's collection languished in storage due to lack of space.

The museum's treasures date back to the Neolithic era (6800 BC) and include antiquities from the Bronze Age, Cycladic, Minoan, Mycenaean and classical periods, with exquisite pottery and frescoes, jewellery and countless other objects from throughout Greece. The sculpture collection, one of the world's most important, includes a colossal 3m 610-BC *kouros* (statue of a male youth) from the sanctuary of Poseidon at Sounion – the oldest existent *kouros*. There are many masterpieces, among them a life-sized Cycladic figurine from Amorgos (the largest ever found), a 2m bronze statue, believed to be Poseidon or Zeus, dating from 460 BC, and a marble statue from Delos (c 100 BC) of Aphrodite with Eros, raising her sandal to ward off a frisky Pan. The extensive Egyptian collection is one of the most important in Europe.

Agamemnon's Death Mask

One of the most popular exhibits is the exquisite Mycenaean gold collection, found in unlooted tombs excavated by Heinrich Schliemann at Mycenae from 1847 to 1876. The finds correspond with Homer's famous tale in the *Iliad* and *Odyssey*. Despite modern dating techniques suggesting it belonged to an earlier king, the 1600-BC gold funerary mask (below) is believed to be Agamemnon's and is a star attraction.

PLAKA & ANAFIOTIKA (9, D2)

Plaka, the historic neighbourhood located under the Acropolis, is a magnet for tourists and Greeks alike – a colourful and lively mix of old Athens with busy restaurants, cafés, tourist shops and galleries. Beyond the busy tourist drag, exploring Plaka's stone-paved narrow streets is a rewarding journey with many significant monuments and ancient, Byzantine and Ottoman ruins providing a palpable sense of history. Cars are limited and the streets are being increasingly made pedestrian-only, adding to the area's charm.

One of Plaka's pleasant surprises is the **Anafiotika** quarter, a picturesque labyrinth of quiet, narrow, windy paths with island-style houses decorated with bougainvillea and bright pots of colour.

The whitewashed Cycladic-style houses were built by homesick stonemasons from the island of Anafi, brought in to build the king's palace during the rebuilding of Athens after independence. It is still home to many of their descendants. The 17th-century **Church of Agios Georgios** (St George of the Rock) marks the entrance to the Anafiotika, with the 1847 **Church of Agios Simeon** to the north.

INFORMATION

- € free
- Ⓜ Syntagma, Akropoli, Monastiraki
- ⓧ Klepsidra (Thrasyvoulou 9; p81); Amalthia Cafe (Tripodon 16)

NEIL SETCHFIELD

Foundations

Many of the Byzantine churches were built on the site of ancient temples in an attempt to crush the Pagan elements of the city – some have visible segments of temples used in the new structure.

Most of the churches in Plaka still operate today, and the traditional Easter services attract people from all over Athens.

Many neoclassical buildings in Plaka have been meticulously restored (the old university of Athens' neoclassical building on the corner of Theorias and Klepsidra is now a museum) as the area has become one of Athens' more exclusive neighbourhoods, popular with artists and intellectuals.

SYNTAGMA SQUARE   (7, D5)

Syntagma (Constitution) Square is crowned by the grand **Parliament House**, originally built as a palace for King Otto, the Bavarian prince installed by the allies after Greek independence. It remained a royal palace until 1935, when it became the seat of the Greek Parliament. Its colourful history includes a stint as a shelter for homeless refugees from Asia Minor.

INFORMATION

- 🖳 www.culture.gr
- ✉ Plateia Syntagmatos, Syntagma
- € free
- 🕑 Parliament library 9am-1.30pm Mon-Fri
- Ⓜ Syntagma
- ♿ good

The Greek Parliament lights the way

Only the library, which often hosts exhibits, is open to the public. In the Parliament forecourt, the **Tomb of the Unknown Soldier**, a monument to the country's fallen, is guarded by the striking *evzones* in traditional uniform. The sculpture of a dying soldier makes a stunning backdrop for the popular changing of the guard ceremony.

The grand square, laid out in 1835 by designers of the new capital, has undergone several face-lifts and remains the centre point of the city.

The historic Grand Bretagne hotel, one of the remaining original buildings, was built in 1862 to accommodate visiting dignitaries, a role it maintains today. The Nazis made it their headquarters during WWII and it was the site of an attempt to blow up Winston Church-

ill on Christmas Eve 1944. The refurbishment of the grand King George II hotel (p96) next door will hopefully counterbalance the McDonald's and fast-food joints that line the other side of the square.

Pom-Pom Parade

The Parliament is guarded day and night by *evzones*, the presidential guards in traditional uniform of short kilts and pom-pom shoes, who stand rigid and stony faced during their shifts. On the hour, every hour, three replacements march up Vasilissis Sofias and arrive for a colourful changing of the guard ceremony. On Sunday and on major holidays, the 6ft-plus *evzones* come out in the full regalia for an extended affair with military band (10.45am). The costume is based on that worn by *klephts*, the rebels of the War of Independence – the red fez symbolises bloodshed and the white kilts have 400 pleats, one for every year of Turkish occupation. *Evzones* groupies can go to the back of the Parliament gardens and the presidential palace (on Irodou Attikou) for more changing of the guard routines.

ANCIENT AGORA (9, B2)

The best-preserved *agora* (market or place of assembly) in Greece gives invaluable insight into the workings of the ancient city. The Agora was the centre of civic life and government, a bustling hub of social activity, housing the law courts and the market. Soc-rates came here to expound his phil-osophy, and in AD 49 St Paul came to win converts to Christianity.

First developed in the 6th cen-tury BC, it was destroyed by the Persians in 480 BC, then rebuilt and flourished until AD 267 when the Heruli, a Gothic tribe from Scandinavia, destroyed it.

INFORMATION

☎ 210 321 0185
💻 www.culture.gr
✉ Adrianou 24,
  Monastiraki
€ €4 (free with
  Acropolis pass)
🕑 8am-7pm (8am-5pm
  Nov-Mar)
ℹ Entrances on
  Adrianou, Thisiou
  & Vrysakiou
Ⓜ Monastiraki, Thisio

There is a useful model of this huge site in the **Agora Museum** in the restored 138-BC **Stoa of Attalos**, which has a significant collection of finds, including a 5th-century terra-cotta water clock used for timing speeches. The 45-column, two-storey stoa was essentially an elite shopping arcade and hang-out for rich Athenians, where they came to watch the Panathenaic procession.

During Byzantine, Frankish and Ottoman eras, the area was covered in houses. The site was excavated and the Stoa of Attalos reconstructed in 1953–56. More than 400 mod-ern buildings were demolished to uncover the Agora.

The **Temple of Hephaestus**, the 'Thisseion' on the western end, was dedicated to the god of metallurgy and was surrounded by foundries and metal workshops. Built in 449 BC, it is the best-preserved Doric temple in Greece, with 36 columns and a frieze on the eastern side depicting nine of the 12 labours of Heracles. The site has many significant ruins and foundations from other buildings, including statues from the Odeon of Agrippa, and the Stoas of Zeus Eleftherios (Freedom), Basileios (Royalty) and Poikile (Painted Stoa), the Metroon (Record Office), prison and the Tholos (where civic dinners were held).

DON'T MISS

- great drain and *in situ*–inscribed boundary stone ('I am the boundary of the Agora')
- fine Byzantine frescoes in the 11th-century Church of the Holy Apostles
- headless statue of Roman emperor Hadrian (below)

BENAKI MUSEUM (6, B3)

Housed in the stunning former home of the Benaki family, this is the oldest private museum in Greece and ranks among its best. It was founded in 1930 by Antonis Benakis, son of the wealthy Alexandrian merchant Emmanuel Benakis, a distinguished family of the Greek diaspora.

The modern museum's vast collection represents the historical and cultural development of Greece and Hellenism. It includes Benakis' eclectic acquisitions from Asia and Europe and pieces from the Byzantine and post-Byzantine eras. It has been the recipient of many significant collections and major donations since it was inaugurated in 1931.

INFORMATION

- ☎ 210 367 1000
- 🖳 www.benaki.gr
- ✉ Koumbari 1 (cnr Vas Sofias), Kolonaki
- € €6
- 🕒 9am-5pm Mon, Wed, Fri & Sat, 9am-midnight Thu, 9am-3pm Sun
- Ⓜ Syntagma
- ♿ good
- ✕ on-site restaurant

Once a Macedonian mansion's reception room, now another breathtaking exhibit at the Benaki Museum

A 10-year, US$20 million renovation completed in 2000 refurbished all the galleries. There is a fine restaurant on the terrace overlooking the National Gardens and the excellent gift shop has been expanded. There is also an impressive new **temporary exhibitions wing** (8, B3; Pireos 138, cnr Andronikou, Thisio).

More than 20,000 items are on display chronologically over four levels, beginning with prehistory and continuing on to the formation of the modern Greek state. It has an excellent Byzantine collection and a gallery focusing on the development of Hellenism during foreign domination.

The spectrum of Greek cultural history is covered, including Karaghiozi shadow puppets, a stunning array of costumes, jewellery, textiles and paintings, which include early works by El Greco.

The antiquities collection includes Bronze-Age finds from Mycenae and Thessaly and Cycladic pottery, while the Egyptian collection includes Greco-Roman *fayum* funerary portraits.

Benakis' heart is immured inside the museum's entrance, but the soul of Greece is well-enshrined in his gift to the country.

DON'T MISS

- Euboia treasure with 3000 BC gold and silver cups
- Mycenaean gold jewellery from Thebes
- two signed El Greco paintings
- two mid-18th-century wood-carved reception rooms from Kozani mansions

LYKAVITTOS HILL (6, C1)

If you are not game to make the steep walk, a funicular railway behind Kolonaki, which runs every 30 minutes, takes you through a tunnel to the peak of Lykavittos Hill. The name means 'Hill of Wolves' but these days there is barely a dog on the rocky crag, which rises 272.7m.

Rising starkly from the sea of apartments below, Lykavittos is the other hill that dominates central Athens, along with the Acropolis. At night the view is spectacular and the air is cool, but even during the day this is a great place to get some perspective on the Athens panorama (pollution and summer haze permitting).

INFORMATION

- ☎ 210 722 7092
- ✉ cnr Aristippou & Ploutarhou, Lykavittos (funicular)
- € €4 return
- ⏰ 9am-11.45pm
- Ⓜ Evangelismos
- ✖ Orizontes (p73); Prasini Tenta café

On a clear day you can see the island of Aegina and the Peloponnese from the top, and wonder why it takes so long to get to the coast when it is not that far at all. There are walking paths through the cypress- and pine-covered hill. An open-air theatre, built in 1964 on a former quarry site on the northern slope, hosts concerts and theatrical performances in summer.

On the summit, the white **Chapel of Agios Georgios**, impressively floodlit at night, stands on the site of an ancient temple that was once dedicated to Zeus. There are two cannons just below on the western side that fire salutes on special occasions. Regular church services are held at the Chapel, the most important being on 23 April, the day of the patron saint, St George, and Good Friday, when there is a moving candlelit procession along the hill.

There's a fine but pricey restaurant (Orizontes; see p73) on the top of the hill, monopolising the superb views, and a café facing the other side. Further down, the shady Prasini Tenta café is a worthy alternative for lunch or a relaxing sunset drink.

Open-Air Concerts

In summer, the **Theatre of Lykavittos**, left, hosts evening concerts and theatre. For events information call **Athens Festival** (☎ 210 722 2092). The open-air amphitheatre is one of the cooler (literally) venues in town, with sensational views from the top rows. The surrounding rock face is often dotted with precariously perched people getting a free show.

NEIL SETCHFIELD

PANATHENAIC STADIUM (7, E7)

The imposing marble stadium built into the eastern side of Ardettos hill was the venue for the first modern Olympic Games in 1896.

The Panathenaic (or Panathenian) stadium was originally built in the 4th century BC by the statesman Lykourgos to host the track events of the Panathenaic games, held in honour of the goddess Athena.

INFORMATION

- ☎ 210 325 1744
- 🖥 www.culture.gr
- ✉ Vas Konstantinou, Mets
- € free
- 🕐 8.30am-1pm & 3.30-7pm
- Ⓜ Syntagma;
- 🚋 2, 4, 11, Stadio stop

NEIL SETCHFIELD

It had a straight track with rectangular seating around it. Under Hadrian's reign, the stadium was reconfigured for gladiatorial contests (1000 wild beasts were once baited in the arena).

Athenian benefactor Herodes Atticus built a new stadium in Pentelic marble that was ready for the AD-144 Panathenaic Festival. It was a Roman stadium with a rounded end and curving sides. An Apollo and Hermes double-headed herm (pillar) that once stood along the central spine of the track is in the National Archaeological Museum (p12).

After years of disuse, during which it was used as a quarry (and much of the marble removed) and gradually covered in debris, the stadium was excavated by Ernst Ziller from 1869 to 1870. Its restoration was undertaken by Anastasios Metaxas according to Ziller's plans, with funds donated by wealthy benefactor George Averoff, whose statue stands by the café.

The work was (almost) completed in 1896 for the first modern Olympic Games. The oval arena seats about 50,000 people and spans 204m x 33m, with a training track at the top.

While the 'Kallimarmaron', as it is widely known, cannot meet the needs of a modern-day Games, it was chosen for the Athens 2004 archery competition – one of the Games' most ancient sports – and the finish of the Olympic Marathon. In 2003, the stadium underwent significant restoration work in preparation for the Games, and to repair damage from the 1999 earthquake.

JOHN BORTHWICK

World's First Marathon

While few sporting events are held at the stadium these days, it is the finish point for the annual Athens Marathon, held on the first Sunday in November. More than 3000 runners from around the world tackle the 42km event, following the historic route run by Pheidippides in 490 BC from the battlefield at Marathon to Athens to deliver the news of victory against the Persians (he immediately collapsed and died of exhaustion).

MUSEUM OF CYCLADIC & ANCIENT GREEK ART (6, B3)

This exceptional private museum houses the biggest private collection of Cycladic art in the world, as well as an impressive collection of ancient Greek art. The museum was custom-built in 1986 for the personal collection of Nicholas and Dolly Goulandris, members of one of Greece's richest shipping families. It was expanded to include bequests and donations and in 1992 took over the stunning 19th-century Stathatos mansion, designed by Ernst Ziller. The two buildings are connected by a glass corridor. Temporary exhibitions are held in the Stathatos wing.

Well displayed, lit and labelled, the museum's collection is presented largely chronologically over four floors. Although it comprises pieces dated to AD 400, the emphasis is on Cycladic civilisation that flourished in the Aegean around the sacred island of Delos from 3200 to 2000 BC.

INFORMATION

- ☎ 210 722 8321
- 🖳 www.cycladic.gr
- ✉ Neofytou Douka 4 & cnr Vas Sofias & Irodotou, Kolonaki
- € €3.50
- 🕒 10am-4pm Mon & Wed-Fri, 10am-3pm Sat
- Ⓜ Evangelismos
- ♿ only from N Douka entrance
- 🍴 on-site café

DON'T MISS

- Cycladic 'Modigliani' c 2800-2300 BC (1st fl, case 1)
- *Drinker* c 2800-2300 BC (1st fl, case 17)
- 5th-century BC water jug (2nd fl, case 24)
- *Athenians at the Symposion* ~d fl, case 32)

The Cycladic collection, displayed on the 1st floor, includes life-sized marble statues, tiny figurines and pottery from the period. The distinctive, white, minimalist slender figurines of the Cycladic era, depicting raw human forms, have long inspired modern artists and sculptors, including Picasso, Modigliani and Henry Moore.

On the fourth floor, the Karolos Politis collection has pieces from the Mycenaean period to the 14th century, including 8th-century-BC Corinthian bronze helmets and fine terracotta vases.

A pleasant atrium café is a great pit stop and the gift shop is well worth exploring.

ROMAN ATHENS (9, C2)

Under Roman rule, the city's civic centre was moved to the **Roman Agora**. The partly excavated site features the foundations of several structures, including a 1st-century, 68-seat public latrine to the right of the entry, and a *propylon* (entrance) on the south-eastern corner.

INFORMATION

☎ 210 324 5220
💻 www.culture.gr
✉ cnr Adrianou &
   Eolou, Monastiraki
€ €2 (free with
   Acropolis pass)
🕑 8am-7pm (8am-5pm
   Nov-Mar)
Ⓜ Monastiraki

Looking for the latrine at the Roman Agora

While some shops have been excavated, the main surviving feature is the well-preserved **Gate of Athena Archegetis**, flanked by four Doric columns, which was erected in the 1st century AD and financed by Julius Caesar.

The octagonal **Tower of the Winds**, next to the Agora, is thought to have predated the Agora, built about 150–125 BC by the astronomer Andronicus. It is considered an ingenious construction, functioning as a sundial, weather vane, water clock and compass. Made of Pentelic marble, it had a bronze triton as a weather vane and reliefs of eight wind figures on each side depicting the wind patterns.

The Tower of the Winds was converted to a church and then used for dervishes under Ottoman rule. (The **Fethiye Djami mosque** on the northern side of the Agora is one of the city's few surviving reminders of Ottoman times.)

Closer to Monastiraki station is the surviving part of the **Library of Hadrian**, once the most luxurious public building in the city. Erected around AD 132, it had an internal courtyard and water feature and was bordered by 100 columns.

Unfortunately, the site is closed to visitors (due to reconstruction work) but you can see the western façade, the ancient entrance and some of the niches of the library in the distance.

Moonlight

During the full moon in midsummer, key archaeological sites in Greece are opened to the public in the evening. The Acropolis is magical to visit by moonlight and should not be missed if you are in Athens. Moonlight concerts in the Roman Agora have also become an annual event. Check the listings in newspapers or the website www.culture.gr.

NATIONAL ART GALLERY (6, D3)

Greece's premiere art gallery has its permanent collection of modern Greek art and sculpture on show in a new wing that opened in 2000 as the gallery celebrated its centenary. A €3.4 million face-lift and extension added 2000 sq metres of exhibition space and installed the latest technology, including an advanced audio system with CD tours in English and Greek.

NEIL SETCHFIELD

The history of Greek art is presented in chronological lines and themes exploring the country's unique art movements. Prize exhibits include three masterpieces from El Greco (Domenicos Theotokopoulos), including *The Burial of Christ*, acquired for US$700 000 in 2000, and *St Peter*.

The art exhibition begins with a small post-Byzantine collection, followed by the Eptanesian school artists, originally from the Ionian islands, who led the transition from Byzantine to secular painting. It then traces the years after independence through to the work of renowned 1930s artists such as Yiannis Tsarouchis and Nikos Hadjikyriakos-Ghikas.

Postwar artists get less wall space, but this will be remedied in the gallery's second stage of expansion; another 6000 sq metres of exhibition space is expected after 2004. The Alexandros Soutzos Sculpture Museum, a new annexe in Goudi, was to open by mid-June 2004.

The gallery also hosts major temporary international exhibitions in the front wing.

DON'T MISS

- Vrysakis' *Exodus from Messolongi*
- Gyzis' *Behold the Celestial Bridegroom Cometh*
- surrealist Engonopoulos' *Delos*
- Lytras' *The Kiss*
- El Greco's *Concert of Angels*

FILOPAPPOS HILL/HILL OF THE PNYX   (7, A7)

Also known as the Hill of the Muses, pine- and cypress-clad Filopappos Hill, southwest of the Acropolis, is a pleasant place for a wander, offering great views of the Acropolis and beyond, to the plains of Attica and the Saronic Gulf.

The Monument of Filopappos

The **Monument of Filopappos** stands on the summit, built in AD 114–16 in honour of prominent Roman governor, Julius Antiochus Filopappos, who is depicted in a frieze driving his chariot.

A fort to defend Athens was built here in 294 BC.

A path next to Dionyssos taverna, on Dionysiou Areopagitou, leads you to the 16th-century **Church of Agios Dimitrios Loumbardiaris** (from the Greek word for cannon), named after an incident in which a Turkish garrison on the Acropolis allegedly tried to fire a cannon on Christians gathered at the church, but the gunners were killed by a miraculous thunderbolt.

Sensitively restored in the 1950s, the church has some fine frescoes and is popular for baptisms and weddings (the adjacent café is a cool retreat with great views). On the first day of Lent, 'Clean Monday', Filopappos is invaded by people picnicking and flying kites, as is customary throughout Athens.

To the north of Filopappos Hill is the smaller **Hill of the Pnyx**. This was the meeting place of the Democratic Assembly in the 5th century BC. Aristides, Demosthenes, Pericles and Themistocles were among the great orators who addressed assemblies here.

Northwest of the Pnyx you'll find the **Hill of the Nymphs**, with the 1840s **Athens Observatory** on the summit.

Further down the hill is the **Church of Agia Marina**, which has a lively annual festival on 17 July, celebrated with a colourful street fair. Filopappos has many other smaller paths for walks and is popular with joggers, but caution should be exercised at night.

Hill of Dance

Since 1965, Filopappos Hill has been the venue for lively performances of traditional Greek music and dance by the renowned **Dora Stratou Dance Theatre** (see p84). The company has given more than 5000 performances before a total audience of more than 2.6 million.

BYZANTINE & CHRISTIAN MUSEUM (6, C3)

With the last stages of a major expansion and modernisation almost complete, the Byzantine and Christian Museum has become one of the city's pre-eminent galleries.

GEORGE TSAFOS

INFORMATION

- ☎ 210 723 2178
- 🖥 www.culture.gr
- ✉ Vasilissis Sofias 22, Athens
- € €1.50, extra charge for special temporary exhibitions
- ☽ 8.30am-3pm Tue-Sun
- ⓘ Closed to spring 2004. Hosts Byzantine & classical concerts in summer.
- Ⓜ Evangelismos
- ♿ free entry (ground floor galleries only)
- ✖ on-site restaurant & café planned

A priceless collection of Byzantine and post-Byzantine art showcases the glory of Byzantium, which is slowly claiming its rightful place as a significant epoch in history after long being overshadowed by ancient Greece.

The museum has been housed in the elegant Tuscan-style villa of the French Duchess de Plaisance since 1930. The permanent collection was to be completely re-organised and moved to a new wing, with the latest technologies and themed displays used to shed light on Byzantine and post-Byzantine culture. A greater selection of the museum's collection of more than 15,000 artefacts from Greece and other reaches of the Byzantine empire will be on display, along with temporary exhibitions.

DON'T MISS

- mosaic icon of the Virgin: *The Episkepsis*
- two-sided, 13th-century icon with St George on the front in gallery 7
- 4th-century sculpture of Orpheus playing the lyre surrounded by animals

Byzantium meets Tuscany

Visitors can see icons from the 9th to 19th century, early Christian sculptures, frescoes, ceramics, wall paintings, exquisite embroideries, jewellery and a precious collection of ecclesiastical vestments and secular items in gold and metal, including the Mytiline treasure.

Along with increased gallery space, there will be a restaurant and café and an amphitheatre for performances. The current gift shop has some exquisite icons.

THEATRES
(9, B3 & C3)

The **Theatre of Dionysos** (9, C3), on the Acropolis' southeastern slope, was built on the site of the Dionysia Festival, during which there were contests, men clad in goatskins sang and danced, and the masses feasted and partied.

The first theatre, built in the 6th century BC, was made of timber. During the golden age, politicians sponsored productions of the dramas and comedies of Aeschylus, Sophocles, Euripides and Aristophanes. Reconstructed in stone and marble by Lykourgos between 342 and 326 BC, the theatre had seating for more than 15,000 spectators, with 64 tiers of seats. Only about 20 survive. An altar to Dionysos once stood in the middle of the orchestra pit. The marble thrones on the lower levels were reserved for dignitaries and priests – the grand one in the centre was for the priest of Dionysos. It is identifiable today by the lion's paws and satyrs and griffins carved on the back. The plebs had to make do with the limestone seating.

The **Theatre of Herodes Atticus** (9, B3) was built in AD 161 in memory of his wife, Regilla, and was one of ancient Athens' last grand public buildings. The semicircular theatre had a cedar roof over parts of the stage and an imposing three-storey stage building of arches.

Relive the drama of ancient times: the Theatres of Herodes Atticus (top) and Dionysos (below)

Excavated in the late 1850s, the theatre was restored in time for the 1955 Hellenic Festival. It remains Athens' premiere, and most inspiring, venue for summer performances of drama, music and dance. The theatre is open to the public during shows (see p84), but is visible from the outside at street level and from above.

DON'T MISS

- 2nd-century-BC relief of Dionysos' exploits (backstage)
- the *Asclepion*
- Stoa of Eumenes, once the promenade for theatre audiences
- a show at the Theatre of Herodes Atticus

TEMPLE OF OLYMPIAN ZEUS (7, D7)

The colossal Temple of Olympian Zeus is the largest in Greece and took more than 700 years to build. The 104 Corinthian columns stood 17m high with a base diameter of 1.7m. Fifteen remain today – one lies on the ground having fallen in a gale in 1852.

Foundations of a small temple dedicated to the cult of Olympian Zeus (dated 590–560 BC) lie on the site. Peisistratos began building a temple twice its size in the 6th century BC, but it was abandoned due to a lack of funds.

A succession of leaders attempted to finish the temple, making adjustments to the original

INFORMATION

- ☎ 210 922 6330
- 🖳 www.culture.gr
- ✉ Vas Olgas, Athens
- € €2 (free with Acropolis pass)
- ☷ 8am-7pm (8am-5pm Nov-Mar)
- Ⓜ Akropoli

plans along the way, which explains inconsistencies in the temple. Hadrian finally took credit for finishing the task in AD 131. The temple had a giant gold and ivory statue of Zeus. In 2001 the temple was the setting for a musical extravaganza by Vangelis, used to launch NASA's Mars space probe.

Hadrian's Arch once linked a thoroughfare heading past **Lysicrates Monument** along the **Street of Tripods**, where 'tripod' trophies were dedicated to Dionysos by winners of ancient drama contests. Made of Pentelic marble, the arch was erected in Hadrian's honour in AD 132, after the consecration of the temple, for which it was a kind of architectural preface. It was also intended to mark the border of the ancient and Roman cities. The inscription on the northwestern frieze reads 'This is Athens, the ancient city of Theseus'. On the other side, it says 'This is the city of Hadrian, and not of Theseus'. The city's best-preserved example of Roman public baths lies west of the Themistoklean city wall in front of Hadrian's Arch.

Lysicrates Monument

The 335–334 BC monument was erected by Lysicrates, a *choregos* (sponsor) of the drama contests, to display the bronze tripod trophies. The circular building, with six Corinthian columns and a frieze showing scenes from Dionysos' life, is the only choregic monument preserved almost complete.

In 1669 it was incorporated into a Capucin monastery and used as a library, in which Lord Byron allegedly wrote part of *Childe Harold*.

KERAMIKOS   (8, D2)

As well as being the largest and best-preserved classical necropolis, the Keramikos cemetery is a little oasis in an otherwise noisy industrial corner of Athens.

It is also the site of the once-massive **Dipylon Gate**, where in antiquity the processions entered the city on their way to the Acropolis via the Ancient Agora. These days you have to search for the plaque which marks the ruins of the gate, but it all starts to make sense as you see the Acropolis ahead.

You can also see the site of the **Sacred Gate** through which pilgrims entered to travel along Sacred Way to Eleusis.

Named after the potter's workshops that once thrived in the area, the cemetery was the burial ground for Athenians from 3000 BC to the 6th century AD. The grand Street of Tombs, where elite Athenians were buried, has some impressive tombs, notably the 4th century BC marble bull in the plot of Dionysos of Kollytos. The one *in situ* is a replica – the original and many other precious finds, including pottery, funerary offerings, toys and even knucklebones sets, are in the **Oberlaender Museum** on the site.

Less visited than many other sites, it is green and peaceful and a delight in spring when the wildflowers are in bloom. Turtles crawl about, while frogs inhabit the spring that runs through the site.

Excavation work for an aborted metro station next to the site (it was diverted after major protests) uncovered a wealth of treasures, including more than 7000 *ostraka* (shards of pottery marked with the names of ostracised Athenian statesmen) that were buried there.

Keramikos Cemetery

Ancient Paths

Athens' key archaeological sites can now be accessed via a network of pedestrian walkways that form the city's 'archaeological park' – a grand route around the centre of classical Athens. The pedestrian precinct begins at the Keramikos site, and continues along the once-busy Dionysiou Areopagitou thoroughfare – transformed into a grand cobbled promenade, lined with cafés – taking you from Thisio past the Ancient Agora, around the southern foothills of the Acropolis, past the theatres all the way to the Temple of Olympian Zeus (see walk p45).

THE COAST   (1, B3)

Despite notoriously hot summers, heading to the coast was never part of the average tourist's itinerary on a short pit stop in Athens, but recent – and continuing – waterfront redevelopment, new green zones and construction of a new tram line are all opening up the sea to the city.

Palio Faliro was Athens' first harbour (Theseus set out from here to Crete to find and kill the Minotaur) and later became a lively summer resort. But for some reason Athens turned its back on the water and the area was largely neglected.

The coast, which stretches from Faliro to Glyfada, was nevertheless a pleasant, if patchy and traffic-clogged part of the city where in summer Athenians would promenade and party at the nightclubs on the beach (which have also been cleaned up in recent years).

INFORMATION

Ⓜ Faliro
🚊 A1 Faliro, A2 Glyfada
€ free

Athen's long-lost coast, as seen from Filopappos Hill

Beach Babies

Athenians have always flocked to the sea in summer, and while there are free public beaches near Athens, the Greeks are not keen on roughing it – thus the institution of organised beaches and beach resorts. Most of the beaches once run by the state or local municipalities have been privatised and upgraded and offer all manner of water sports, sun lounges, cafés, playgrounds, beach volleyball facilities and even kabanas. Some of the best are Astir Beach, Voula and Vouliagmeni (see p116).

One of the Olympics' greatest legacies is the redevelopment of the Faliro coastal zone (the biggest waterfront project in Europe, bigger than Barcelona's Olympics effort), which includes a huge pedestrian overpass leading to a waterfront leisure and entertainment precinct, with restaurants, open-air theatres and cultural and sporting events.

The new tram line will run from the city centre to the coast at Faliro, then veer either left towards Palio Faliro or continue down a scenic beachside route to Glyfada, past esplanades, cafés, bars, beaches, playgrounds and marinas. On the way are the redeveloped Agios Kosmas Sailing Centre area and the former Hellinikon airport, which will become a massive municipal park after the Olympics.

Glyfada is renowned for its shopping and fine restaurants, while summer nightspots stretch all the way along the picturesque drive to Varkiza.

While some disruption is expected post-Olympics as temporary venues are removed and landscaping completed, the area will no doubt become a highlight of the city, especially in summer.

KAISARIANI MONASTERY (1, B2)

The lush forest and gardens surrounding the 11th-century monastery of Kaisariani, nestled on the slopes of Mt Hymmetos, make this a wonderful

NEIL SETCHFIELD

INFORMATION

- ☎ 210 723 6619
- ✉ Mountain road starting at Ethnikis Antistaseos, Kaisariani
- € €2
- ☾ 8.30am-2.45pm Tue-Sun (grounds open sunrise-sunset)
- ⓘ Ticket booth sells postcards & CDs of Byzantine music
- 🚌 20 min trip
- 🚌 take bus 223 or 224 buses from Akadimias, then 2km uphill walk from terminus
- ✗ bring a picnic

sanctuary in the city. Athenians come here for picnics and walks and despite being only 5km from town it's so peaceful; you cannot see or hear the sprawling city below.

Much of the pine forest was destroyed during WWII and the monastery itself had long crumbled into ruin. It was restored in the 1950s and reforested by the Athens Society of the Friends of the Trees.

Dedicated to the Presentation of the Virgin, the monastery was built on the foundations of an ancient temple; four columns from the temple support the church's dome.

The walled complex has a central court around which are the kitchen and dining rooms (closed after being damaged in the 1999 earthquake), the monks' cells and the bathhouse.

The *katholikon* (main church) is built in cruciform style, highlighted with a dome. Most of the well-preserved frescoes on the walls and ceiling date back to the 17th and 18th centuries. The church has two services each year: the Presentation of the Virgin on 21 November and the colourful Epitaph ceremony on Good Friday, at 3pm. The earliest frescoes, on the narthex, were painted in 1692 by Ioannis Hypatios from the Peloponnese. The adjacent chapel dedicated to Agios Antonios and the belltower are later additions.

In its heyday in the late 12th and early 13th centuries, it was a cultural centre with 300 monks. They were spiritual leaders, made thyme honey and wine and kept a rich library (destroyed by the Turks during the War of Independence). The monastery enjoyed considerable privileges and survived Frankish and Ottoman occupation.

Athenians once came here to drink from the 'magical' springs

DON'T MISS

- the ram's head marble fountain outside, spouting spring water
- the makeshift chapel above the picnic grounds

to aid fertility, but the water is low and undrinkable these days. Up along a trail past the picnic grounds, there is a makeshift chapel, full of icons, votive offerings and candles, in the ruins of an early Christian basilica and Frankish church.

Sights & Activities

MUSEUMS

Given its wealth of history and culture, it is not surprising that Athens has more than 130 museums, exploring everything from pottery and antiquities to botany and the history of the quarry. Some are more sophisticated and hi tech than others but each provides endless insight into the country's rich past and present obsessions.

Centre of Folk Art & Traditions (9, D2)
The rooms in the mansion of famous folklorist Angeliki Hatzimichalis, built in the 1920s, have been set up to depict the traditional pastoral Greek way of life, including an old kitchen and its stove and utensils and ceramic plates from Skyros. The museum also has a chapel, regional costumes, embroideries, weaving machines, ceramic vases and family portraits.
☎ 210 324 3972
✉ **Hatzimihali Agelikis 6, Plaka** € **free** ⏲ **9am-1pm & 5-9pm Tue-Fri, 9am-1pm Sat & Sun**
Ⓜ **Akropoli; Syntagma**

City of Athens Museum (7, C4) Once the residence of King Otto and Queen Amalia (while the royal palace was being built), the museum contains some of the royal couple's personal items and furniture – including the throne. Covering the history of Athens from the end of the Middle Ages to today, the rich displays include paintings by leading Greek and foreign artists and models of 19th-century Athens.
☎ 210 324 6164
🖥 **www.athenscity museum.gr**
✉ **Paparigopoulou 5 & 7,**

Panepistimio € **€5**
⏲ **9am-1.30pm Mon, Wed, Fri & Sat (winter also Sun)**
Ⓜ **Panepistimio**

Epigraphical Museum (7, D2) This important museum, on the site of the National Archaeological Museum, houses the world's most important collection of Greek inscriptions. It is in effect a 'library of stones' detailing official records, lists of war dead, tribute lists showing annual payments by Athens' allies, and the decree ordering the evacuation of Athens before the 480 BC Persian invasion.
☎ 210 821 7637
🖥 **www.culture.gr**
✉ **Tositsa 1, Exarhia**
€ **free** ⏲ **8.30am-3pm Tue-Sun** Ⓜ **Viktoria**
♿ **good**

Ilias Lalaounis Jewellery Museum (7, B7) The talents of Greece's renowned jeweller are showcased in this private museum, with pieces inspired by various periods in Greek history and displays demonstrating the ancient art from prehistoric times. Videos explain the jewellery-making process, while goldsmiths demonstrate ancient and modern techniques. Tours in English are available.
☎ 210 922 1044
🖥 **www.lalaounis -jewelrymuseum.gr**
✉ **Kallisperi 12 (cnr Karyatidon), Makrigianni** € **€3, free 3-9pm Wed & 9-11am Sat** ⏲ **9am-4pm Mon & Thu-Sat, 9am-9pm Wed, 11am-4pm Sun**
Ⓜ **Akropoli**

Who was Venizelos?

Contrary to some tourists' musings, El Venizelos was not a Spaniard mate of El Greco. Eleftherios Venizelos, whose name graces the airport (and thus the signs all over Athens) and other public spaces, was Greece's leading 20th-century politician, with several stints as prime minister during a turbulent period. If you really want to find out more, there are two museums dedicated to him (in Eleftherias Park and at Christou Lada 2, Athens; ☎ 210 322 1254).

Museum Costs & Opening Hours

All state-run museums and archaeological sites offer free admission on Sunday from 1 November to the end of March, the first Sunday of April, June and October and on 6 March, 18 April, 18 May, 5 June and the last weekend in September. Anyone under 18 gets in free year-round, as do card-carrying EU students and fine arts or classics students. Students with an International Student Identity Card (ISIC) get a 50% discount. Families can also get discounts at some museums and galleries.

Most museums and sites are closed on Monday. Key archaeological sites such as the Acropolis are now open from 7am to 7pm. The €12 admission fee for the Acropolis is valid for four days and covers the Ancient and Roman Agoras, Temple of Olympian Zeus, Keramikos and Dionysos Theatre.

Islamic Art Museum

(8, E2) A new annexe of the Benaki Museum, this progressive museum (to open in spring 2004) has been created to house the Benaki's celebrated collection of Islamic art – one of the finest in the world. The neoclassical complex of buildings in Keramikos also incorporates the Centre for the Study of Islamic Civilization.
☎ 210 367 3000
🖥 www.benaki.gr
✉ Agion Asomaton 22 (cnr Dipylou), Keramikos
🕐 9am-5pm Mon & Wed-Sat, 9am-3pm Sun
Ⓜ Thisio

Jewish Museum

(9, E2) One of the most important in Europe, this modern museum traces the history of the Romaniote and Shephardic Jewish community in Greece from the 3rd century BC. The impressive collection includes religious and historical artefacts, documents, folk art and costumes. Nearly 90% of Greece's Jews, most of whom lived in Thessaloniki, were killed during the Holocaust.
☎ 210 322 5582
🖥 www.jewish museum.gr ✉ Nikis 39, Plaka Ⓔ €3
🕐 9am-2.30pm Mon-Fri, 10am-2pm Sun
Ⓜ Syntagma

Kanellopoulos Museum

(9, C2) The imposing 1884 mansion on the northern slope of the Acropolis houses the Kanellopoulos family's extensive collection, donated to the state in 1976. It includes jewellery, clay-and-stone vases and figurines, weapons, Byzantine icons, bronzes and *objets d'art*

dating from every period of Greek history.
☎ 210 321 2313
✉ Theorias 12 (cnr Panos), Plaka Ⓔ €2
🕐 8.30am-3pm Tue-Sun
Ⓜ Monastiraki

Maria Callas Museum

(8, C2) A collection of memorabilia, photographs, correspondence, clothing and personal belongings from the revered late Greek-American opera diva, who died heartbroken in 1971 after Aristotle Onassis dumped her for Jackie O. This small museum is in the impressive complex in Athens' old gasworks (see p39).
☎ 210 346 0981
🖥 www.technopolis.gr
✉ Pireos 100, Gazi
Ⓔ free 🕐 10am-4pm Mon-Fri Ⓜ Thisio
♿ good

Find your inner diva at the Maria Callas Museum

Museum of Cypriot Antiquities (8, B1)

Greece's only museum of Cypriot antiquities has an impressive display of rare finds from the civilisation that flourished on Cyprus from prehistoric to medieval times. The distinctive pieces, part of the Pierides collection, are well displayed in this modern, private museum within the Athinais complex.

☎ 210 348 0000
💻 www.athinais.com.gr
✉ Kastorias 34-36, Votanikos, Gazi €️ €3
🕑 9.30am-10pm 🚌 813 from Pireos, Omonia to Sidera stop ♿ excellent

Museum of Greek Costume (6, A3)

Part of the Lyceum of Greek Women, the museum presents excellent thematic exhibitions from its comprehensive collection of regional costumes, jewellery and accessories. There are also 23 porcelain dummies that belonged to Queen Olga, all in traditional dress. The gift shop sells interesting books on folk culture, calendars and handmade crafts.

☎ 210 362 9513
✉ Dimokritou 7, Kolonaki €️ free
🕑 10am-1pm Mon, Wed & Fri (closed Aug)
Ⓜ Syntagma

Museum of Greek Folk Art (9, E2)

This state-owned museum founded in 1918 moved to Plaka in 1973. It has examples of folk art from 1650 to the present, including elaborate

Rock on at the Museum of Greek Popular Instruments

embroidery, weaving, costumes, shadow-theatre puppets, silverwork and wood and stone carvings. The 2nd floor has a reconstructed traditional village house and fine wall murals by renowned primitive artist Theophilos Hatzimichail.

☎ 210 322 9031
💻 www.culture.gr
✉ Kydathineon 17, Plaka
€️ €2 🕑 10am-2pm Tue-Sun Ⓜ Syntagma

Museum of Greek Popular Instruments (9, C2)

More than 1200 folk instruments dating from the 18th century are on display over three floors, with headphones allowing visitors to listen to the music of the *gaida* (Greek goatskin bagpipes), Byzantine mandolins and more. The 1842 mansion is also home to the Research Centre for Ethnomusicology and its extensive archives. Recitals of Greek music are often held in the garden.

☎ 210 325 0198
💻 www.culture.gr
✉ Diogenous 1-3, Plaka
€️ free 🕑 10am-2pm Tue & Thu-Sun, noon-6pm Wed Ⓜ Monastiraki

Museum of Traditional Greek Ceramics (9, C1)

An annexe of the Museum of Greek Folk Art, the museum features folk pottery and hand-painted ceramics from the first two decades of the 20th century, collected by professor Vassilil Kyriazopoulos. It is housed in the mosque *(tzami)* built by the city's governor, Tzisdarakis, in 1759 (its minaret has been removed).

☎ 210 324 2066
✉ Areos 1, Monastiraki
€️ €2 🕑 9am-2.30pm Mon & Wed-Sun
Ⓜ Monastiraki

Museum of 20th Century Design (1, C2)

Fans of 20th-century interior design will love this museum, charting the evolution of modern furniture by leading names such as Le Corbusier, Dali, Gaudi and Frank Lloyd Wright, to name a few. If you're truly inspired, you can always purchase pieces from the museum's retail store.

☎ 210 685 0611
✉ Patmou 4-12 (Technal Plaza), Maroussi €️ free
🕑 9am-6pm Mon & Wed, 9am-8pm Tue, Thu & Fri, 10am-3pm Sat Ⓜ Irini

Almost enough for a coffee, Numismatic Museum

National Historical Museum (7, D5)

Since 1962, Greece's first parliament has housed memorabilia from the War of Independence, including Byron's helmet and sword, weapons, costumes and flags. There are also paintings, Byzantine and medieval exhibits, photos, and royal portraits illustrating Greece's evolution since Constantinople's fall in 1453.
☎ 210 323 7617
✉ Stadiou 13, Plateia Kolokotroni € €3, free Sun ☾ 9am-2.30pm Tue-Sun Ⓜ Syntagma

Nautical Museum of Greece (5, C5)

This expansive museum brings Greece's maritime history to life, with models of ancient and modern ships, seascapes by some of Greece's greatest 19th- and 20th-century painters, guns, flags and maps. There are machine guns from old warships, anchors and part of a submarine on the museum's grounds.
☎ 210 451 6264 ✉ Akti Themistokleous, Freatida

Sq, Zea Marina, € €2 ☾ 9am-2pm Tue-Fri, 9am-1.30pm Sat Ⓜ Piraeus, then bus 904 ♿ good

Numismatic Museum (7, D5)

Even if you have no interest in coins, it is worth visiting this exemplary neoclassical building, once home of renowned archaeologist Heinrich Schliemann, who excavated Troy and Mycenae. There are some beautiful frescoes and mosaic floors, along with the highlights of the museum's 600,000-strong collection, considered one of the top five in the world.
☎ 210 364 3774
✉ Panepistimiou 12, Syntagma € €3
☾ 8.30am-3pm Tue-Sun Ⓜ Syntagma ♿ good

Philatelic Museum (7, E6)

Stamp collectors will love this small museum, featuring the history of philately and post offices in Greece. Exhibits range from old mailboxes and scales to postmen's uniforms and the 1886 printing plates from the first stamp designed by the Hellenic Postal Service, featuring a bust of Hermes – and naturally a huge stamp collection.
☎ 210 751 9066
✉ Fokianou 2 & Plateia Stadiou, Mets ☾ 8am-2pm Mon-Fri € free
Ⓜ Syntagma 🚌 2, 4, 11

Piraeus Archaeological Museum (5, C2)

This museum showcases antiquities from Piraeus, Attica, the Saronic Gulf and the island of Kythera, including finds

from a Minoan sanctuary on Kythera. Star attractions are the four colossal bronzes, including a life-sized 520-BC statue of Apollo.
☎ 210 452 1598
✉ Harilaou Trikoupi 31, Zea Marina, Piraeus € €3 ☾ 8.30am-3pm Tue-Sun 🚌 040 from Syntagma ♿ excellent

Theatre Museum (7, D4)

A fine collection of memorabilia from great moments of 19th- and 20th-century Greek theatre, from costumes worn in ancient dramas to dressing rooms dedicated to opera diva Maria Callas and actress Melina Mercouri, and a tribute to renowned director Karolos Koun. There are stage sets painted by leading Greek artists, props, photographs and programmes.
☎ 210 362 9430
🖥 www.theatre-museum.gr ✉ Akadimias 50, Athens € free
☾ 9am-2pm Mon-Fri Ⓜ Panepistimio

War Museum (6, C3)

The junta-era museum honouring the armed forces has fighter planes in the forecourt that you can climb into. Inside, there is an invaluable historical collection of war memorabilia from the Mycenaean period to the present, including weapons, maps, armour and models of battles.
☎ 210 724 4464
✉ Rizari 2 (cnr Vasilissis Sofias), Athens € free
☾ 9am-2pm Tue-Sun Ⓜ Evangelismos ♿ good

NOTABLE BUILDINGS & MONUMENTS

Athens Town Hall (7, C4)

The 1874 town hall was abandoned for modern premises in the early 1980s, but following a major restoration the mayor's office moved back to its historic home in 1995. The chambers have stunning frescoes by leading artists Fotis Kondoglou and George Gounaropoulos, as well as a valuable collection of art on display.

☎ 210 331 2420-2
🖥 www.cityofathens.gr
✉ Athinas 63 (opposite Plateia Kotzias), Athens
€ free ⏲ 8am-3pm
Ⓜ Omonia

Gennadius Library (6, C2)

In 1922 businessman turned diplomat John Gennadius handed over his personal library of books on Greece (comprising more than 27,000 volumes) to the American School of Classical Studies. The fine neoclassical library, purpose-built to house the collection, has a stunning reading room and a fine art and memorabilia collection.

☎ 210 721 0536
🖥 www.ascsa.edu.gr/gennadius/genn.htm
✉ Souidias 61, Kolonaki
€ free ⏲ 9am-5pm Mon-Fri, 9am-2pm Sat
Ⓜ Evangelismos

National Theatre of Greece (7, B3)

Designed by Ernst Ziller and completed in 1901, the decorative columned façade of the National Theatre was inspired in part by Hadrian's Library;

Plato takes a break outside the Athens Town Hall

the interior was based on Vienna's People's Theatre. It served as the Royal Theatre exclusively for the king's guests until 1908. The building, damaged in the 1999 earthquake, was closed for renovation until spring 2004. For performance details, see p84.

☎ 210 522 0585
🖥 www.n-t.gr ✉ Agiou Konstantinou 22, Omonia
Ⓜ Omonia

Building Boom

The grandiose neoclassical trilogy of buildings on Akadimias is part of the legacy of the Hansen brothers, Theophile and Christian, the Danish architects who joined the neoclassical building frenzy after independence.

Flanked by the two giant columns on which Apollo and Athena stand, the **Athens Academy** is considered Theophile's most impressive work in Greece. Completed in 1885, it was paid for by the Austro-Greek Baron Sina. The exquisite frescoes in the entrance depict the myth of Prometheus.

The ostentatious buildings were built using white Pentelic marble and incorporate highly decorative friezes. The more modest senate house of the **Athens University** in the middle was designed by Christian. Theophile's staircase of griffins leads to the 1902 **National Library** (6, A2; ☎ 210 338 2541; Panepistimiou 28-32, Panepistimio; ⏲ 9am-8pm Mon-Thu, 9am-2pm Fri & Sat), which has a stunning reading room.

Bathe in the Ottoman past at the Turkish Baths

Presidential Palace & Megaron Maximou (7, E6) The imposing former royal palace designed by Ernst Ziller in the 1870s, guarded by two *evzones*, is now the offical residence of the president of the Hellenic republic. The prime minister's official residence, an elegant but less palatial neoclassical building down the road, is regularly guarded by a media throng. Unfortunately, admission is by invitation only.
☒ **Irodou Attikou**
Ⓜ **Syntagma**

Turkish Baths (9, C2) The only surviving public bathhouse in Athens – and one of the few remnants of the Ottoman period – the refurbished 17th-century bathhouse of Abit Efendi gives some insight into the era's rituals. Beyond the steams and scrubs, bathhouses were also an important meeting point.
☎ 210 3244340
☒ **Kyrristou 8, Plaka**
€ free ☽ 10am-2pm Wed & Sun
Ⓜ **Monastiraki**

BYZANTINE CHURCHES & MONASTERIES

Agios Nicholas Rangavas (9, D2) The 11th-century Byzantine church was part of the palace of the Rangava family, which included Michael I, emperor of Byzantium. The church bell was the first installed in Athens after liberation from the Turks (who banned them) and was the first to ring in 1833 to announce the freedom of Athens. It now hangs inside the church and is rung every year on 25 March.
☎ 210 322 8193 ☒ Prytaniou 1 (top of Epimarchou) ☽ 8am-noon & 5-8pm Ⓜ Akropoli

Paying Your Respects

Always dress respectfully when entering a church. The custom is to light a beeswax candle for yourself and your loved ones, making a small offering in the boxes provided.

The silver *tamata* (votive offerings) around icons represent special prayers, thus the depictions of different parts of the body when someone is ill, or a baby for childless couples (or Volkswagen Beetle, as found in one souvenir shop).

Easter is the biggest Greek Orthodox celebration in Greece and a busy period for Plaka's historic churches.

Try to catch a night-time service in the week before Easter, particularly on Palm Sunday, Easter Thursday or Easter Saturday.

Athens Cathedral & Little Metropolis (7, C5) The ornate 1862 Athens Cathedral dominates the square on Mitropoleos, and is the archiepiscopal Greek Orthodox church of Athens. However, far more significant, both historically and architecturally, is the small 12th-century **Church of Panagia Gorgoepikoos** (Virgin Swift to Hear) next to the cathedral. Known as 'Little Metropolis', the cruciform-style church was built from marble, and used reliefs and pieces of ancient and early Christian monuments. It is built on the ruins of an ancient temple.
☎ 210 322 1308
☒ **Plateia Mitropoleos, Monastiraki**
☽ 7am-7pm, Sun Mass 6.30am
Ⓜ **Monastiraki**

The *fanouropita* cake at Panagia Grigoroussa, Taxiarhon and Fanouriou will help you find your way home

Church of the Holy Apostles of Solakis (9, B2)

One of the oldest churches in Athens, built c AD 1000, this Byzantine church is on the site of the Ancient Agora. During the period of Ottoman rule it underwent many changes, but was restored in the 1950s. The church contains frescoes transferred from the demolished Agion Spyridon.

✉ Ancient Agora
🕙 8am-7pm Tue-Sun (8.30am-3pm Dec-Mar)
Ⓜ Monastiraki; Thisio

Dafni Monastery (1, A2)

One of the most splendid Byzantine monuments in Greece, the 11th-century Dafni Monastery's mosaics are considered masterpieces of the era. Its closure, after damage caused by the 1999 earthquake, was the last in a long history of blows for the monastery – it's been sacked by crusaders, desecrated by Turks, occupied by Gothic Cistercian monks, destroyed by antipagan edicts of emperors and later turned into a barracks and mental institution.

☎ 210 581 1558
✉ Iera Odos, Haidari
🕙 closed 🚌 A16 from Koumoundourou Sq

Kapnikarea (9, D1)

Right in the middle of the pedestrian shopping strip of Ermou is the Byzantine church of Kapnikarea, dedicated to the Presentation of the Virgin Mary. Completed in the 13th century, the cruciform-style domed church was nearly destroyed to make way for progress. It now belongs to the Athens University, which undertook its restoration.

☎ 210 322 4462
✉ Kapnikareas (cnr Ermou), Monastiraki
🕙 8am-1pm Mon-Sat, 5-8pm Tue, Thu & Fri, 8-11.30am Sun
Ⓜ Monastiraki

Panagia Grigoroussa, Taxiarhon & Fanouriou (9, C1)

Every Saturday afternoon, worshippers arrive at this Plaka landmark for a special service to get their *fanouropita* cake blessed before sharing it with passers-by. The cake is supposed to help you find something lost or someone you may be seeking. It tastes pretty good, too.

✉ cnr Taxiarhon & Epaminonda (near Andrianou), Monastiraki 🕙 5.45pm Apr-Oct; 4.45pm Nov-Mar
Ⓜ Monastiraki

Give thanks for your trip at the Athens Cathedral

Sotira Lykodimou (9, E2)
The largest medieval structure (and only octagonal Byzantine church) in Athens has served as the Russian Orthodox Church since 1847. Built in 1031, it was bought and restored by Tsar Nicholas 1 in the 1850s, while Tsar Alexander II added the belfry at the end of the 19th century.
✉ **Filellinon (near Kydathineon)** ☉ 7-10am Ⓜ **Monastiraki**

ART GALLERIES

Greek art is not just the domain of the ancients. Athens has an active contemporary arts scene and numerous private, commercial and public galleries exhibiting local and international artists. Many new galleries have opened in (or older ones relocated to) warehouses in the emerging arts precinct around Psiri and Omonia.

A.Antonopoulou.Art (8, F1) An impressive new art space opened by Angeliki Antonopoulou, who's been in the gallery business for 20 years. Designed by leading architect Aris Zampikos, the gallery has great views of Psiri and focuses on contemporary Greek artists.
☎ 210 321 4994
🖳 aaart@otenet.gr
✉ **Aristofanous 20, 4th fl, Psiri** € free
☉ 4-9pm Tue-Fri, 12-4pm Sat Ⓜ Monastiraki

Athens Municipal Art Gallery (8, E1)
The municipality's rich collection includes more than 2300 works from the leading 19th- and 20th-century Greek artists, with strong representation from the '30s generation, who created some of the masterpieces of Greek art. The gallery also boasts a fine collection of engravings.
☎ 210 324 3023/22
✉ **Pireos 51, Koumoundourou Sq, Athens** € free
☉ 9am-1pm & 5-9pm Mon-Fri, 9am-1pm Sun Ⓜ Thisio

Bernier/Eliades Gallery (8, D3) A leading Athens gallery, which showcases prominent Greek artists and also brings exhibitions from an impressive range of international artists, from abstract American impressionists to British pop and performance team Gilbert and George.
☎ 210 341 3935
🖳 www.berniereliades.gr
✉ **Eptahalkou 11, Thisio** € free ☉ 11am-8pm Tue-Fri, noon-4pm Sat Ⓜ Thisio

Deste Foundation, Centre for Contemporary Art (1, B2) Founded by international contemporary art collector Dakis Ioannou, the Deste centre has a popular restaurant, art shop and bar frequented by the arts set. Designed by New York architect/designer Christian Hubert, the former paper warehouse hosts major exhibitions of Greek and international artists.
☎ 210 672 9460
🖳 www.deste.gr
✉ **Omirou 8, Neo Psihiko** € free ☉ 10am-6pm Mon-Fri, noon-4pm Sat Ⓜ Ethniki Amina, then 🚌 A6, A7, B6, B7 (Faros stop) or 🚌 550, 450 from the Panathenaic Stadium ♿ good

Frissiras Museum (9, E3)
This private museum of contemporary European paintings, housed in two beautifully renovated neoclassical mansions in Plaka, showcases more

---

Psiri On Line
The innovative website www.psirri.gr has a useful directory of Psiri's ever-growing number of trendy galleries and restaurants, as well as special exhibitions and other happenings.

Athens Municipal Art Gallery: a treasure-trove of Greek art

than 3000 works of art, focusing mainly on the human figure, and a café. The historic building at No 7 was designed by an unknown student of Ernst Ziller.

☎ 210 323 4678 ▯ www.frissiras museum.com ✉ Monis Asteriou Tsangari 3 & 7, Plaka € €6 ☽ 11am-7pm Wed & Thu, 11am-5pm Fri-Sun Ⓜ Syntagma Ⓖ good

Gounaropoulos Museum (6, F3) The former home and studio of one of Greece's revered modern painters is now a museum displaying his paintings and some of his personal effects. George Gouna-ropoulos (1889–1977), known as Gounaro, worked in Greece and Paris. His distinctive, dream-like work has been inspired by French and German impressionists.

☎ 210 777 7601 ✉ Gounaropoulou 6, Zografou € free ☽ 9am-1pm & 6-9pm Tue-Thu (5-8pm Oct-Mar), 10am-2pm Fri-Sun 🚌 taxi

Ileana Tounta Contem-porary Art Centre (6, D1) This leading gallery, recently expanded and refurbished, has two exhibition halls, an art shop and a pleasant café overlooking a lovely garden. Tounta has an established record of hosting eclectic exhibitions of international and Greek artists.

☎ 210 643 9466 ▯ www.art-tounta.gr ✉ Armatolon Ke Klefton 48, Lykavittos € free ☽ 11am-7pm Tue-Fri, 11am-3pm Sat Ⓜ Ambelokipi Ⓖ good

National Museum of Contemporary Art (7, B8) The landmark former Fix brewery is being trans-formed into the capital's first comprehensive modern art museum, showcasing works by Greek and foreign artists. Until it reopens after 2004, exhibitions are being held in the new art space at the Megaron Moussikis (p84).

☎ 210 924 2111-2 ✉ Kallirrois (cnr Frantzi), Fix € €3 ☽ 11am-7pm Tue, Wed & Fri-Sun, noon-10pm Thu ⓘ free tours 12pm Sun &

7pm Thu Ⓜ Syngrou-Fix Ⓖ good

Pierides Museum of Con-temporary Art (4, A1) Dimitris Pierides founded this museum, in a stunning mansion, for his collection of more than 1000 paintings, sculptures, engravings and ceramics, mostly by post-WWII artists from Greece and Cyprus. There's also a library of modern Greek art.

☎ 210 898 1729/1167 ✉ Vasiliou Georgiou 29, Glyfada € free ☽ 9am-2pm Mon-Fri (6-8.30pm for special exhibitions), 10am-2pm Sat & Sun 🚕 A2 🚌 A2 5th stop Glyfada

Rebecca Camhi Gallery (8, F1) A visionary who led the art scene's move into the warehouses of gritty downtown Athens, Camhi continues to present eclectic exhibitions of contemporary art from leading inter-national artists.

☎ 210 383 7030 ▯ www.rebeccacamhi .com ✉ Sofokleous 23, Omonia € free ☽ by appointment Ⓜ Omonia

PARKS & PUBLIC PLACES

Areos Park (7, D1)
The city's biggest park, just north of the Archaeological Museum, can be a good place to escape the madness during the day. Among its wide tree-lined avenues is a long line of statues of War of Independence heroes. It is not recommended at night, when it is frequented by vagrants and shady characters.
✉ **Alexandras (cnr 28 Oktovriou-Patission), Pedion Areos** € **free** Ⓜ **Viktoria** ♿ **good**

Eleftherias Park Arts Centre (6, D2) The old army barracks used as a prison during the junta era have been converted into two galleries, which are used for temporary art exhibitions. The park is also home to the Venizelos Museum (p37), dedicated to the great statesman, and a pleasant café-restaurant.
☎ **210 723 2603** ✉ **Vasilissis Sofias (Eleftherias Park), Ambelokipi** € **free** ⏱ **9am-1pm & 5-9pm Tue-Sat, 9am-1pm Sun** Ⓜ **Megaro Moussikis**

National Gardens (7, E6)
The former royal gardens, designed by Queen Amalia around the palace that is now the Parliament, are a great green refuge during the summer. Winding paths lead to ornamental ponds with waterfowl and a botanical museum, which has interesting drawings, paintings and photographs.

Byron's Greek holiday romance was more intense than most: Zappeio Gardens

The café near Irodou Attikou is a pleasant spot for a break.
☎ **210 721 5019** ✉ **Amalias, Syntagma (next to Parliament)** € **free** ⏱ **7am-dusk** Ⓜ **Syntagma** ♿ **good**

Omonia Square (7, C3)
The architects just can't seem to get poor Omonia right. They were back to the drawing board after public outcry over the uninspiring square unveiled in 2002, which had no trees and

Supreme View

The massive Ancient Agora is best appreciated from above. The ideal bird's-eye view is from **Areopagus Hill**, which you reach from just below the Acropolis entrance.

Areopagus was the site of the supreme court where murder, treason and corruption trials were heard before the Council of the Areopagus.

This is where St Paul delivered his famous sermon in AD 51 and gained his first convert, Dionysos, who became the patron saint of Athens.

endless concrete. The once grand square is a transport and business hub by day and hang-out for the seedier elements of the city by night. The jury is still out on the fate of the square for 2004.

Ⓜ Omonia Ⓔ free

Technopolis (8, C2)

One of the most interesting of Athens' many recent redevelopments has been conversion of the 1862 gasworks into a unique heritage industrial site and cultural centre. The old furnaces and other indus-trial features have been maintained, along with the different stone build-ings that once made this a thriving self-contained community, including a carpenter's shop, smelter, garage, restaurant, barber-shop and clinic. It regularly hosts multimedia exhibi-tions, concerts and special events.

☎ 210 346 0981
🖥 www.technopolis.gr
✉ Pireos 100, Gazi
Ⓔ free 🕓 9am-9pm Mon-Fri during exhibi-tions Ⓜ Thisio 🔾 good

Zappeio Gardens (7, D6)

Next to the National Gardens, the Zappeio's formal gardens surround the majestic palace built in the 1870s by the wealthy Greek-Romanian benefac-tor Konstantinos Zappas. It was used as the head-quarters of the Olympic Committee for the 1896 Olympics, held opposite at the Panathenaic Stadium (p18). Unless there's a

function on, the guards will let you in for a look at the stunning courtyard. The gardens are not closed at night, and in summer the historic Aigli outdoor cinema (p92), bistro (p78)

and Bedlam bar (p90) make this a cool place to hang.

✉ **Amalias, Syntagma (next to Parliament)**
Ⓔ free Ⓜ **Syntagma**
🔾 **good**

Athens First National Cemetery

In a city with limited open space, the old **cem-etery** (7, E8; ☎ 210 923 6118; Anapafseos, cnr Trivonianou, Athens; 🕓 7.30am-7pm May-Sep, 8am-5pm Oct-Apr; 🚌 4) is a pleasant, if quirky, place to enjoy a stroll through the well-tended gardens and resting place of many rich and famous Greeks and philhellenes. The lavish tombstones and mausoleums include works of art by leading Greek sculptors of the 19th century, including *The Sleeping Maiden* by Halepas, on the tomb of a young girl.

The mausoleum of archaeologist Heinrich Schliemann is decorated with Trojan War scenes from reliefs he discovered during excavations.

The Mother of the Occupation, a bronze statue (near the entrance) of a starved woman clutching a baby to her breast, is a moving memorial for the 40,000 citizens who died during WWII.

NEIL SETCHFIELD

QUIRKY ATHENS

Limni Vouliagmeni (1, C3)
The source of the water at this lake has never been found, as some divers have lost their lives discovering. But the lake is popular with winter swimmers who enjoy the constant 22°C temperature of part-salt/part-spring water, which has therapeutic mineral qualities. It's a wonderful setting, with its sheltered rock face, manicured lawns and old-style café-bar, frequented by a regular crew of elderly citizens in their bathrobes and bathing caps. Its gradual slope makes it good for kids.
☎ 210 896 2239
✉ Limni Vouliagmeni
€ €5 ☽ 7am-7pm summer, 7am-5pm winter
🚌 A2 (or E2 express in summer) to Plateia Glyfada & then 🚌 114
✕ on-site café-bar

Ancient Shipsheds (5, D2)
In the exposed basement of an ordinary Piraeus apartment block are the ruins of three slipways from an ancient shipshed in Piraeus. Zea was the main base for the Athenian fleet, which had more than 196 shipsheds (the ancients used to drag their ships in to shore). In a great example of preserving the past while getting on with life, the ruins can be seen next to the pylons holding up the apartment block. It is lit at night and visible from the street.
✉ Sirangiou 1 (cnr Akti Moutsoupoulou), Piraeus
€ free 🚌 20, Sirangiou stop 🚻 good

Hellenic Cosmos
Take a virtual reality trip into ancient Greece at this hi-tech interactive **museum** (8, B3; ☎ 210 483 5300; www.fhw.gr/cosmos; Pireos 254, Tavros; ☽ 9am-4pm Mon, Tue & Thu, 9am-8pm Wed & Fri, 10am-3pm Sun; Ⓜ Kalithea; € varies; 🚻 excellent). Enter the Kivotos time machine – with floor-to-ceiling screens – and go back 2000 years to a 3D ancient Miletus, the Temple of Zeus at Olympia or the world of Greek costume.

A second 'magic screen' introduces you to the art of the traditional olive press and ancient Olympic sports. The centre is part of the Foundation of the Hellenic World. English guides are available on request.

Tom's Garden (9, E2)
Tucked behind the main drag of Plaka, this temple to innovative and artistic recycling and political commentary has been making passers-by do a double take for years. The mysterious Tom has turned a vacant lot into an ever-changing display of art which, on last sight, had been painted pink with an elephant at the wheel of an old VW Beetle (Taliban Taxi Service).
✉ Sotiras (cnr Iperidou),

Who knew recycling could look so good?

Plaka € free
Ⓜ Syntagma

St John the Baptist of the Column (8, F1)
It is easy to miss this little church, set in a courtyard in downtown Athens. Its name comes from the incongruous Corinthian marble column that sticks out from the roof. While some believed it came from a gymnasium, another theory is that it once stood alone and supported a Roman statue. The church (1844) was built around it during the Byzantine period, when it became a talisman believed to have magical healing properties. On 29 August people come here to perform a ritual from that time, when fever patients attached a waxed thread to the column to transfer the fever to the column.
✉ Evripidou (cnr Menandrou), Athens ☽ 7am-3pm Ⓜ Monastiraki

ATHENS FOR CHILDREN

Allou Fun Park (1, B2) Not exactly Disneyland, but the closest you'll get in Greece to a theme park. This giant entertainment zone has more than 20 amusement rides and thrills for young and old, snacks and occasional live shows.
☎ **210 425 6999** ✉ **Kifissou (cnr Petrou Ralli), Renti** € **€2-4 per attraction** 🕑 **5pm-1am Mon-Fri, 10am-2pm Sat & Sun** 🚊 **21 to Kan Kan stop**

Battleship Averoff (1, B3) This restored battleship, now permanently moored at Faliro, was the fastest ship in the Greek fleet between 1910 and 1920 and played a pivotal role in the Balkan Wars. Visitors can tour the ship from the engine room to the captain's quarters, along with exhibits detailing the ship's history.
☎ **210 983 6539** ✉ **Trocadero Marina, Palio Faliro** € **€1** 🕑 **summer 9am-1pm & 3-5pm Mon, Wed & Fri, 9am-1pm Tue & Thu, 11am-3pm Sat & Sun; winter 11am-1pm & 4-6pm Mon, Wed & Fri, 11am-3pm Sat & Sun** Ⓜ **Piraeus, then** 🚌 **909 to Oelen stop**

Children's Art Museum (9, E2) Founded to cultivate a love of art and creative development, this museum is one of few of its kind. There are exhibitions of young artists' work and workshops for children to let their creative juices flow.
☎ **210 331 2621** 💻 **www.childrensartmuseum.gr** ✉ **Kodrou 9, Plaka** € **€2, children free** 🕑 **10am-2pm Tue-Sat, 11am-2pm Sun (closed Aug)** Ⓜ **Syntagma**

Children's Museum (9, D2) More playschool than museum, this delightful and innovative interactive centre has a range of activities to encourage children's development and engage the imagination, such as a popular chocolate-making session. Most of the activities are suitable for non-Greek speakers.
☎ **210 331 2995-6** 💻 **www.hcm.gr** ✉ **Kydathineon 14, Plaka** € **free** 🕑 **10am-2pm Tue-Fri, 10am-3pm Sat & Sun** Ⓜ **Syntagma**

Museum of Natural History (3, B1) Promoting the natural sciences and protection of Greece's wildlife habitats and endangered species, this museum has exhibits of all sorts of animal and plant life, fossils and other scientific displays. It was being revamped by early 2004. Their modern and innovative GAIA Centre around the corner has interactive displays.
☎ **210 801 5870** 💻 **goul@gnhm.gr** ✉ **Levidou 13, Kifissia** € **€3** 🕑 **9am-2.30pm, Sat-Thu** Ⓜ **Kifissia**

Railway Museum (7, B1) Though not strictly for children, the collection of old steam locomotives, mine trains, wagons, royal carriages and trams here is sure to appeal to kids at heart. Highlights include an 1899 steam locomotive and passenger car from the famous rack railway of Diakofto–Kalavrita, and the smoking car of the train of the sultan of Abdul Aziz.
☎ **210 524 6580** ✉ **Liossion 301 & Siokou 4, Sepolia** € **free** 🕑 **9am-1pm Mon-Fri, 5-8pm Wed, 9am-1pm Sun** Ⓜ **Sepolia**

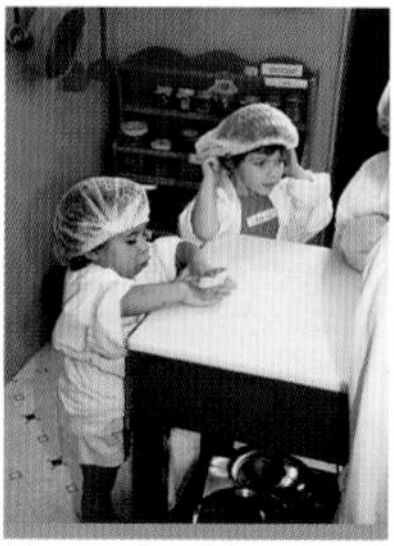

They start work young at the Children's Museum

Spathario Museum of Shadow Theatre (1, C2) This exhibition of the famous Karaghiozi and his colourful band of shadow-theatre puppets was founded in 1965 by Eugene Spatharios. The collection dates back to 1947. There are also Greek and English books on shadow theatre.
☎ **210 612 7245** ✉ **cnr Vas Sofias & Ralli (Kastalias Sq), Maroussi** € **free** 🕑 **10.30am-1.30pm Mon-Fri & Sun, 5.30-7.30pm Mon & Wed** Ⓜ **Maroussi, or** 🚌 **A7, B7**

WORTH THE TRIP

Some interesting museums and significant archaeological sites are just outside Athens and are worth visiting if time permits. They can be a bit hard to do by public transport but are popular with hard-core archaeology buffs. Some sites can also be combined with a swim at a nearby beach.

Eleusis (1, A2) The sanctuary of Demeter is one of the most fascinating ancient places in Greece, site of cult worship and Eleusinian mysteries celebrating the goddess Demeter and her daughter Persephone. On the coast 22km west of Athens, it's now in the middle of an industrial wasteland. The on-site museum has some significant finds and a good model of the site.
☎ 210 554 6019
🖳 www.culture.gr
✉ Gioka 1, Eleusis 3
€ €3 ⏲ 8.30am-3pm
🚌 Athens–Corinth Hwy to Elefsina 🚌 A16 or B16 from Koumoundourou Sq (1hr)

Koutouki Cave (1, C3)
Although facilities here have seen better days, the cave itself – one of the finest in Greece – is a pleasant surprise. Discovered by a shepherd in 1926 after his goat fell down a tiny hole (the only natural entrance to the cave), it was excavated and opened to the public. You can tour the two-million-year-old cave's stalactites and stalagmites, with a sound and light show finale. It's not far from the airport and Vorres Museum.
☎ 210 664 2910
🖳 www.culture.gr
✉ Peania Cave € €4.50
⏲ 10am-3.30pm

ℹ 30min-tours every 30min 🚗 4km

Marathon (2, D2) The site of one of the most famous battles of all time – in which the outnumbered Athenians defeated the 25,000-strong Persian Army – was being made over for the Olympic marathon at the time of research. There is also a tomb to the fallen, and a museum in town.
☎ 229 405 5155
✉ 114 Plateon, Marathonas (site ☎ 229 405 5462)
€ €3 ⏲ 8.30am-3pm Tue-Sun 🚌 (KTEL) Marathonos from Mavromateon (☎ 210 823 0007, departs every hr) to Tymvos, then short walk (2hr)

Ramnous (2, D1) The museum's displays include the restored entablature and western pediment of the 5th-century Temple of Nemesis, goddess of divine retribution, and a large statue of the goddess, reconstructed from hundreds of fragments. The site itself has ruins of a fortress, buildings, graves and other temples. There are some coves nearby for a swim.
☎ 229 406 3477
🖳 www.culture.gr
✉ Ramnous € €2
⏲ 8am-5pm 🚌 (KTEL) Marathonos from Mavromateon (☎ 210 823

0007, departs every 2hr), Agia Marina crossing, then 3km walk (1hr)

Vravrona (2, D2) The Sanctuary of Artemis was a revered site for worshippers of the goddess of the hunt, protector of women in childbirth and newborns. The temple is one of several notable monuments from this Neolithic settlement. The museum houses exceptional finds from the sanctuary and excavations in the area.
☎ 229 908 1274, 229 9027 020 🖳 www .culture.gr ✉ Vravrona
€ €2 ⏲ 8.30am-3pm Tue-Sun Ⓜ Ethniki Amina, then 🚌 304 to Loutsa & taxi 10min (1hr)

Vorres Museum (1, C2)
This private modern art and folk museum is set on a lovely 2.5-hectare estate. Vorres built his home here in 1963 and began collecting art (housed in a modern gallery), furniture, artefacts, textiles and historic objects from around Greece to preserve the national heritage.
☎ 210 664 2520
🖳 www.culture.gr
✉ Parodos Diadohou Konstantinou 4, Peania
€ €4.50 ⏲ 10am-2pm Sat & Sun, Mon-Fri by appointment Ⓜ Ethniki Amina, then 🚌 308 to Koropi-Peania

Out & About

WALKING TOURS
City Highlights

Begin at **Parliament House** (**1**; p14), about 10 minutes before the hour if you want to catch the changing of the guards. Cross over to the historic **Grand Bretagne** (**2**; p96) hotel, turn right at Stadiou, following it until you come to the old parliament building, now the **National Historical Museum** (**3**; p32).

An imposing statue of War of Independence hero Theodoris Kolokotroni points down Omirou. Follow it to Panepistimiou, one of Athens' most impressive boulevards of grand buildings. Cross over to the St Denis Catholic Cathedral and the unusual 1847 Byzantine-style **Eye Hospital** (**4**).

Statues of Apollo and Athena stand above the **Athens Academy** (**5**; p33) on towering columns. Next door is **Athens University** (p33) and the stunning **National Library** (p33) with its marble-columned entry and murals in the portico. Continue up Panepistimiou to busy **Omonia Square** (**6**; p38), which is getting a major face-lift. Cross to the left and head down Athinas, towards the markets of Athens. Pass the restored 1874 **Town Hall** (**7**; p33) and Plateia Kotzia.

The smell of olives, cheese and spices hits you as you approach Athens Central market. Go past the colourful **meat market** (**8**; p54), an Athenian landmark. Turn left at Evripidou and right into Eolou, a pleasant pedestrian walk leading to the Tower of the Winds (p20), below the Acropolis.

On the way you pass the churches of **Agia Chrysospiliotissa** (**9**) and Agia Irini. Stop at café **Aiolis** (**10**; p78) for a break before hitting the shops on Ermou or continuing to Pandrosou into the heart of Monastiraki.

distance 3km **duration** 1½hr
▶ **start** M Syntagma
● **end** M Monastiraki

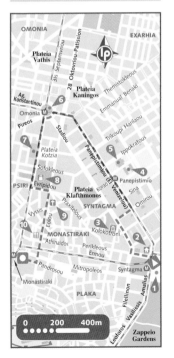

Evzones on a walking tour of Athens

Historic Centre

From **Parliament House** (**1**; p14) cross over Syntagma Square and turn right at Mitropoleos and left into Nikis to enter the Plaka. The pedestrian area starts at Kydathineon. Stop at the **Museum of Greek Folk Art** (**2**; p31), opposite the Church of Metamorphosis.

Tourists and pigeons alike admire Parliament House

Turn right at Adrianou, left at Flessa where the pedestrian way ends, and right again on Kyrristou, past the **Turkish Baths** (**3**; p34), to the octagonal, and ingenious, **Tower of the Winds** (**4**; p20).

Follow the **Roman Agora** (**5**; p20) around and turn right into Peikilis toward the **Stoa of Attalos** (**6**; p15). Turn left at Vrysakiou and walk up the steps along the **Ancient Agora** (**7**; p15) to the foot of the Acropolis. Turn right towards the old Supreme Court foundations on **Areopagus Hill** (**8**; p38), and carefully climb the slippery worn marble steps for a sensational view of Athens.

Turn back along Theorias past the **Kanellopoulos Museum** (**9**; p30) until you get to Agios Simeon Church. Walk around the back of the church (small opening on right), to get to the winding paths of the **Anafiotika quarter** (**10**; p13).

At the church of St George of the Rock, turn into the terraced park and walk out the gate down past Rangavi. To your left the path leads to the Church of Agios Nikolaos Rangava. Turn right into Tripodon and stop at the cute Amalthia café or keep going until you get to the **Lysicrates Monument** (**11**; p25).

distance 3.2km **duration** 2hr
▶ **start** Ⓜ Syntagma
● **end** Ⓜ Syntagma

Turn left into Herefontos and left at the next corner, which leads you Plateia Filomoussou, where you can stop at one of the cafés for a well-earned break.

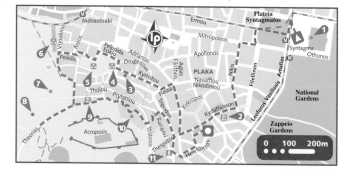

Ancient Promenade

From Monastiraki station, turn into Areos at the **old mosque** (**1**; p20), now a ceramics museum, pass **Hadrian's Library** (**2**; p20) and turn right into Adrianou, walking alongside the perimeter of the **Ancient Agora** (**3**; p15) and the Thisseion. At Plateia Thisiou, turn left and continue along Apostolou Pavlou, passing the expanse of cafés along the promenade that winds around in the shadow of the **Acropolis** (**4**; p9).

When you pass the Filopappos Hill turn-off and entrance to the Acropolis, turn left into Dionysiou Areopagitou and head towards the **Theatre of Herodes Atticus** (**5**; p24) and the **Theatre of Dionysos** (**6**; p24) until you come to the end of the pedestrian precinct. Cross the road and walk to **Hadrian's Arch** (**7**; p25), along the walls of the imposing **Temple of Olympian Zeus** (**8**; p25). Keep on walking along Vas Olgas until you reach the **Panathenaic (old Olympic) Stadium** (**9**; p18).

Cross back over and walk through the cool Zappeio gardens, past the **Zappeio palace** (**10**; p39), stopping at **Aigli café** (p78) for a cool drink and, if you're lucky, some live jazz, or continue to the end of the gardens and turn right at Amalias to get back to **Syntagma Square** (**11**; p14).

distance 4.3km **duration** 3hr
▶ **start** Ⓜ Monastiraki
● **end** Ⓜ Syntagma

They don't build them like they used to, Temple of Olympian Zeus

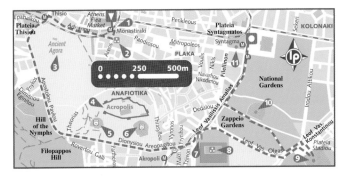

Filopappos Hill

Start at **Parliament House** (**1**; p14), walking along the gardens to the statue of Byron courting Hellas. Cross over at Vas Olgas and walk around **Hadrian's Arch** (**2**; p25), crossing Amalias at the start of the pedestrian section of Dionysiou Areopagitou.

Walk along the promenade past the **Theatres of Dionysos** (**3**; p24) and the **Theatre of Herodes Atticus** (**4**; p24) below the Acropolis until you get to the kiosk at the start of Apostolou Pavlou.

Turn left along the path up the hill towards the church of **Agios Dimitrios Loumbardiaris** (**5**; p22). Follow the path to the right and walk to the **Pnyx theatre** (**6**; p22).

Head back along the path until you get to the wider paved road heading to the path leading to the **Filopappos monument** (**7**; p22) on the summit. The eye-level views of the Acropolis make this one of the best spots for photographers. Head back down the steps to the café next to the church.

distance 3.2km **duration** 2hr
▶ **start** Ⓜ Syntagma
● **end** Ⓜ Akropoli

Now, which way do I go after the Theatre of Herodes Atticus?

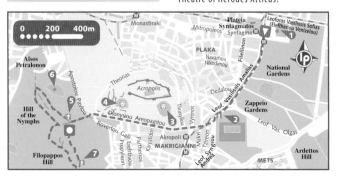

DAY TRIPS
Delphi   (2, C1)

The ancient Greeks regarded Delphi as the centre of the world; according to mythology, Zeus released two eagles at opposite ends of the world and they met here at Delphi.

When you stand at the Sanctuary of Apollo in this spectacular setting, you can sense that this is indeed a special place. Pilgrims once came here (around the 4th century BC) seeking the wisdom of Apollo's oracle. It was thought to be literally the mouthpiece of the god.

These days, the visitors are mostly tourists exploring the sanctuary and expansive archaeological sites. The refurbished museum has an excellent collection of finds from the site, including the celebrated life-sized bronze charioteer, whose piercing eyes follow you around the room.

If you come by car, visit the nearby skiing village of Arachova or head down to the seaside village Galaxidi for fresh fish at one of the seafront tavernas (about 30 minutes drive).

INFORMATION
178km northwest of Athens

- Terminal B Liossion 260 (☎ 210 831 7096, €11, 3hr)
- ☎ 226 508 2312 (museum)
- 🖥 www.culture.gr
- € €6
- 🕑 summer 7.30am-7.45pm; winter 7.30am-5.30pm (museum open 8.30am-2.45pm). Partially closed for renovations until the Olympics.
- ℹ Delphi tourist office (☎ 226 508 2900; Vasileon Pavlos & Fredirikis; 🕑 7.30am-2.30pm Mon-Fri) Hire a car or take an organised tour.

Delphi, centre of the world

Audience members at Delphi's theatre found it hard not be distracted by the view

Cape of Sounion (2, D2)

The Temple of Poseidon is one of the most spectacular ancient sites in Greece, perched on the craggy cliffs of Cape Sounion, with the Aegean Sea making the perfect backdrop.

Cape Sounion is best appreciated early in the morning or late in the afternoon, when the tourist buses have gone and you can stick around for the stunning sunsets. In summer you can stop off along the coast for a swim.

INFORMATION

70km southeast of Athens

- 🚌 from Mavromateon (cnr Alexandras & 28 Oktovriou-Patission), Areos Park (☎ 210 823 0179)
- ☎ 229 203 9363
- 🖥 www.culture.gr
- € €4
- 🕑 summer 10am-dusk, winter 9am-5pm

Built in the 5th century BC on the site of previous sanctuaries, this is where the ancient Greeks worshipped the god of the sea. So inspired was Lord Byron when he visited the temple in 1810 that he carved his name in one of the columns. Sixteen of the 36 Doric columns have been preserved and there are also the remains of a fortification wall, a gateway, arcade and a smaller Temple of Athena.

Nafplio (2, C2)

A popular weekend retreat, the beautiful seaside town of Nafplio is heritage protected. Its old quarter is a wonderful mix of Greek, Venetian and Turkish architecture and the port is lined with stunning neoclassical buildings.

The imposing Palamidi Venetian fortress on the high cliffs above the town is an 800-step climb or a short taxi ride up, and it's worth it just for the view over the Gulf of Argos.

Briefly the capital of Greece during the War of Independence, Nafplio has been a major port since the Bronze Age. It is a charming place to visit, with many cafés, bars and restaurants along the pretty harbour, two other fortresses and plenty of sights to warrant a day trip.

INFORMATION

146km southwest of Athens

- 🚌 Terminal A (Kifissou 100), departs on the hr
- ☎ 275 202 8036 (Palamidi fortress)
- 🖥 www.culture.gr
- ✉ Nafplio
- € €4 (Palamidi fortress)
- 🕑 summer 8am-6.45pm; winter 8am-4.45pm (Palamidi fortress)
- ℹ Nafplio's main tourist office (☎ 275 202 4444; 25 Martiou; 🕑 9am-1pm & 4-8pm) & the tourist police (☎ 275 202 8131) are on the same street. In June Palamidi hosts a folk music festival.

This view of Nafplio is well worth the 800-step climb

Ancient Olympia (2, B3)

With the 2004 Olympics in Athens, interest in where it all began is reaching a peak. Ancient Olympia, in the western Peloponnese, is experiencing a bit of a renaissance and an influx of visitors. Cruise ships are now calling at the upgraded port of Kyllini, the new Athens–Patras highway has shortened the trip and some major hotels have been built on the coast nearby. In 2003 the site museum was closed for a welcome refurbishment.

Ancient Olympia is one of the largest and most impressive archaeological sites in Greece, and is situated in an idyllic lush setting in the Alfios Valley.

The sprawling site, once a walled sanctuary *(altis)*, includes the ruins of a 2nd-century-BC gymnasium, administration buildings, wrestling school, and a newer stadium built for the Panhellenic Games, with the judges' thrones in the middle.

Among the many temples and structures is the showpiece Doric Temple of Zeus, which once housed a gold and ivory statue considered one of the seven wonders of the world.

The Olympia museum has many important exhibits, including sculptures and statues from the Temple of Zeus and the famous well-preserved 4th-century-BC statue of Hermes. The site is well worth a lengthy visit.

Hydra   (2, D3)

The island of Hydra, in the Saronic Gulf, is adored by artists and writers, and you can see why as soon as you enter the picturesque harbour. Gracious stone and whitewashed mansions line the surrounding hillside, which is naturally shaped like an amphitheatre.

Adding to its charm is that fact that Hydra doesn't allow any cars or bikes (except for sanitation and construction vehicles) to drive on or around the island, so donkeys are the only means of transport.

Most of the action in Hydra is concentrated around the great waterfront cafés and shops, leaving the upper reaches viturally deserted. There is also a maze of winding streets to get pleasantly lost in.

The historic Lazaros Kountouriotis mansion on the hill has been turned into a wonderful museum under the auspices of the National Historical Museum.

INFORMATION

50km or 38 nautical miles from Piraeus

- Minoan Flying Dolphins run up to nine hydrofoil services daily from Piraeus in summer & less frequently in winter (☎ 210 419 9000; 1½hr; one-way €16.60). Piraeus Port Authority (☎ 210 412 4585 or 210 411 7341) for Saronikos daily ferry (8am).
- ☎ 229 805 2205 (Hydra Tourist Police)
- 🖳 www.compulink.gr/hydranet
- ✉ Hydra

Boats and donkeys are Hydra's only transport options

ORGANISED TOURS

Most organised-tour companies offer similar services and are normally booked through hotels, or cater to package tourists. The day tours of Athens usually involve a drive-by tour of the sights stopping at one or two key places, such as the Acropolis and its museum, so make sure you are clear on what you will actually get to visit. Sights in Athens are easy to get to on your own so, in many cases, the only real advantage is the guide. The night tours are pretty tacky and really aimed at tour groups. The best-regarded companies are Hop In Sightseeing and Chat.

Archaeological Tours

The **Panhellenic Guides Federation** (☎ 210 322 9705; fax 210 323 9200; Apollonos 9A) can organise private tours by accredited guides to archaeological sites, with prior notice (expect to pay about €90 for four hours). Tour guide **Rania Vassiliadou** (☎ 210 940 3932; raniavassiliadou.virtualave.net), provides a well-regarded service around Athens' archaeological sites and day trips further afield, including Delphi, for groups of up to six people.

Classicist and archaeologist Andrew Farrington and anthropologist Vassiliki Chrysanthopoulou provide personalised tailor-made **cultural introductions to the city** (☎ 210 689 3828; www.atheniandays.co.uk; one hour tours per group €50 to €70) and surrounds, including tours of archaeological sites for up to six people per tour.

Tours to **Delphi** (p47) include the archaeological site and museum and traditional village-cum-ski town, **Arachova**, famous for handmade carpets and quilts. The **Mycenae** tour includes stops at the **Corinth** canal, tomb of Agamemnon and other sights, lunch at Mycenae, a visit to **Nafplio** (p48) and the ancient theatre of **Epidauros**. Tours cost around €80 for a full day.

> ### Wine Tours
>
> Wine tourism is a relatively new phenomenon in Greece. The **Attica Wine Growers Association** (☎ 210 353 1315; www.enoaa.gr) provides information and organises tours of local wineries participating in the Wine Roads of Attica programme. It has an information booth in the arrivals terminal at the airport. The tours visit picturesque vineyards not far from Athens, and are an ideal way to spend a day outside the city.
>
> The 30-hectare **Ktima Evharis** (☎ 210 924 6930, 229 609 0346; www.evharis.gr; Megara, 64km from Athens; ☻ 9am-4pm Mon-Fri, weekends by appointment) is one of the best visitor-friendly wineries near Athens, with a reception centre, tastings and tours, as well as an extensive modern art collection.

Boat

A day cruise to the nearby islands of **Hydra** (p50), **Poros** and **Aegina** can be fun and usually includes a buffet lunch and onboard tourist entertainment with traditional dancing. **Chat Tours'** (p52) one-day cruise (7.30am to 7.30pm, €80) stops at Hydra first, with time for a stroll or swim, and sails to Aegina (via Poros, but you barely have time to get off the boat), where for an extra charge you can take an excursion to the Temple of Aphaia. **Hop In Sightseeing** (p52) does the same route in reverse with lunch on board (7.30am to 7pm, €80).

Walking

Free walking tours of the city's major archaeological sites, galleries and landmarks are held each weekend by the **City of Athens** (☎ 210 324 0762; 10.30am Sunday and every second Saturday, October to June). The tours are conducted in Greek, but guides usually also speak English and other languages. There are different destinations around town you can choose from.

Classic tour territory, Areopagus Hill

TOUR COMPANIES

Chat Tours
The Athens Sightseeing Tour drives past the Tomb of the Unknown Soldier outside Parliament, the Panathenaic Stadium and several other key sites but the only stops are at the Temple of Olympian Zeus and the Acropolis, where you get a reasonable guided tour (9.15am to 12.30pm, €44.50).

There are also half-day afternoon tours (2.30pm to 7pm, €30) that take you along the coastal road to the Temple of Poseidon at **Cape Sounion** (p48).

☎ 210 323 0827
🖳 chat@chatours.gr
✉ Xenofontos 9, Syntagma

Fun Train
A cheat's way of seeing the sights, this little open-air mini-train weaves its way through the narrow streets of Plaka and the Thisio–Acropolis district. It's fun for big kids, too, if the passengers are any indication. The Fun Train departs from the Tower of the Winds near the Roman Agora, but it's best to call **Hop In** for directions and bookings.

€ 40min ride €5
🕑 summer 11am-7pm

GO Tours
Catering to big tour groups, this company has huge offices, and provides the predictable itinerary of short tours to archaeological sites within Athens, as well as longer day trips.

☎ 210 921 9555

A Bird's-Eye View
You don't see choppers very often, but you can take half-hour **Helicopter Tours** (contact Hop In Sightseeing, see below; per person from €660; min 2 passengers; runs during daylight hours only, includes hotel pick-up). The tour flies over the city giving you an aerial view of the sights (though you can't fly over the Acropolis), including the new Olympic complexes. The deluxe Eurocopter twin engine helicopters fly low (3000ft) for optimum viewing.

✉ Athanassiou Diakou 20, Makrigianni 🕑 6am-9pm

Hop In Sightseeing
Unlike other operators, Hop In runs a Hop In–Hop Out tour that allows you to get on and off the bus and check out sites at your leisure over two days. The city tour includes a stop at Parliament House, where people can get off, see the changing of the guard, check out the underground metro and hop back on. You can also add a two-hour guided visit to the National Archaeological Museum. Tours must be booked early on the morning of the same day or, preferably, the day before.

☎ 210 428 5500 (office open 6.30am-10pm)
🖳 www.hopin.com
✉ Zanni 29, Piraeus
€ adult/under 12 from €44/22
🕑 8am-2pm
ⓘ Pick up from hotel

Key Tours
Offers the usual selection of tours, the most popular and best organised being the half-day Athens City Tour (€44) and the afternoon trip to **Cape Sounion** (p48; 3pm to 7pm; €30). The Athens-by-night Tour is a trip around town and then a visit to a taverna in Plaka (€49).

☎ 210 923 3166
✉ Kallirrois 4, Mets
🕑 7am-8pm (office hrs)

Shopping

There are plenty of temptations for shopaholics in Athens, from wonderful handicrafts to exquisitely made shoes and jewellery.

Fashion-conscious Greeks have high disposable incomes and an almost unhealthy consumer zeal, leading to a strong presence of big-name brands and designers. New stores are constantly opening in an increasingly sophisticated market. Harrods and Lafayette were expected to open in mid-2004.

Worry for sale, Monastiraki Fleamarket

Shop 'til You Drop

Trading hours in Athens are still influenced by the old days when people went home for lunch and a siesta during the heat of the day. The family-run shops reopened in the evenings, which is still the best time to shop in summer. But times are changing and many stores now open all day, especially in the busy centre and on the main shopping strips.

Official trading hours are: Monday, Wednesday and Saturday 9am to 3pm; Tuesday, Thursday and Friday 9am to 2.30pm and 5pm to 8.30pm (winter 5pm to 8pm). Department stores open Monday to Friday 8am to 8pm, and Saturday 9am to 6pm.

These hours do not apply to tourist shops, which are usually open until late and on Sunday.

The most concentrated shopping strip is on Ermou, from Syntagma to Monastiraki, which must have more shoes per square metre than any other place in the world.

Top boutiques are mostly scattered around Kolonaki; elite designers and jewellers, including Louis Vuitton, Pentheroudakis and Bulgari, are on Voukourestiou. Kifissia and Glyfada also offer great shopping, with top designers and stores, in a more relaxed environment.

Plaka and Monastiraki are full of souvenir and gift stores that open until late. You can fit in a full day of museums and sights (or business) and still have time to buy souvenirs or spoil yourself with a unique piece of Greek jewellery.

The following guide is by no means definitive but suggests a range of stores to cover most needs, plus a few standout favourites.

Be warned, some sales assistants are a little in your face, greeting you with a terse 'parakalo', (a 'can I help you?' equivalent with a 'what do you want?' tone) and following you around the store. That said, most are friendly, speak English and are happy to assist.

During sale times (July to August and January to February) there are some great bargains. Haggling is acceptable (and effective) in smaller, owner-run stores, particularly souvenir and jewellery shops (especially if you pay cash), but don't bother in major chains or department stores.

DEPARTMENT STORES

Fokas (9, E1) This five-storey department store in a restored neoclassical building in the hub of Ermou stocks a select range of men's, women's and children's wear labels, as well as travel goods, accessories, swim wear, beauty products, toys and books. There's a café on the top floor. There's a second store at Stadiou 41, Omonia, ☎ 210 325 7800.
☎ 210 325 7740
✉ Ermou 11 (cnr Voulis), Syntagma Ⓜ Syntagma

Hondos Center (7, C3) This major chain's 10-level superstore has just about everything, from designer clothes to sunscreen, plus an extensive range of swim wear, cosmetics and perfumes. It's particularly worth a visit during the sales. The rooftop café has great views.
☎ 210 522 1335

Omonia Sq: no trees, but plenty of department stores

✉ Omonia Sq 4, Omonia Ⓜ Omonia

Notos Galleries Lambropoulos (7, C3) Boasting more than 400 shops in the one store, Lambropoulos is one of Athens' oldest department stores, with Greek and imported labels in clothing, footwear, cosmetics and household goods.
☎ 210 324 5811

✉ Eolou 2-8, Omonia Ⓜ Omonia

Marks & Spencer (7, C5) This reliable UK chain has a number of stores in Athens if you're looking for those familiar basics, especially underwear and more conservative clothing.
☎ 210 324 0804
✉ Ermou 33, Syntagma Ⓜ Syntagma

MARKETS

Athens Central Food Market (7, C4) The hectic, colourful Athens *agora* (market) is the highlight of the Athinas market strip. A visual and gastronomic delight with the most amazing range of olives, spices, cheeses and deli treats leads you to the meat market, which can look quite surreal, with hanging carcasses illuminated by endless rows of swinging light bulbs. The fresh fruit and vegetable market is nearby and

there are some gems in the surrounding streets, including many old-style tavernas (see Diporto, p74).
✉ Athinas (btwn Sofokleous & Evripidou), Omonia ⏰ 7am-3pm Mon-Sat Ⓜ Omonia

Monastiraki Flea Market (8, F3) Athens' colourful flea market takes place Sunday, when traders spill out around Plateia Avyssinias and along Adrianou to Thisio. It isn't what it used to

be, but it still has a distinctly festive atmosphere, and the nearby cafés and restaurants are always brimming. There are certainly some bargains, interesting collectables and kitsch delights to be found among the junk. The permanent antique, furniture and collectables stores have plenty to sift through, although it may be better to go during the week. This is the place to test your haggling skills.
✉ around Ifestou &

To Market, to Market...

Almost every neighbourhood in Athens has its weekly street market known as the *laiki,* where you get the cheapest and best variety of fresh fruits and vegetables and household goods.

The city's biggest **laiki** (7, A9; Lagoumitzi, Neos Kosmos; ☼ 7am-2.30pm Sat; Ⓜ Neos Kosmos) is held just behind the Athanaeum Intercontinental on Syngrou, on either side of the Lagoumitzi street overpass (and even on it).

The stalls around the St Analipsis Church sell everything from bed linen, underwear, tools and glassware to old cameras and bric-a-brac.

Pandrosou, Monastiraki
☼ 7am-3pm Sun
Ⓜ Monastiraki

Piraeus Flea Market
(5, C1) This busy Sunday market spreads out along the streets around Piraeus railway station, with merchants selling everything from cheap clothing and shoes to tools and blankets. It is not strong on crafts, and for antiques and collectables, you're better off venturing out during the week when you don't have to fight the crowds to get to the area's excellent selection of antique shops.
✉ around Alipedou, Great Harbour, Piraeus
☼ 7am-2pm Sun
Ⓜ Piraeus

CLOTHING

GREEK DESIGNERS
Afternoon (6, B2) Located just under the St George Lycabettus Hotel, this stylish boutique exclusively stocks up and coming and established Greek designers, including Deux Hommes, Smaragdi, Maro Zannia, Pavlos Kyriakides and Vasso Consola.
☎ 210 722 5380
✉ Dinokratous 1, Kolonaki ☼ closed Sat & Sun Ⓜ Evangelismos

Bettina (6, B3) The pond in the entrance with the faux water lilies leads to three more understated levels of top-name fashion for all ages, including creations by London-based up-and-comer Sophia Kokosalaki, Angelos Frentzos and other well-known Greek and international designers.
☎ 210 323 8759
✉ Pindarou 40 (cnr Anagnostopoulou), Kolonaki
Ⓜ Syntagma

Christos Veloudakis (6, B3) A dramatic-looking boutique, the long red velvet curtains and racks of clothing are both designed for maximum impact. Women's and men's day-and-night wear with an edge.
☎ 210 364 1764
✉ Tsakalof 22a, Kolonaki Ⓜ Syntagma

Elina Lebessi (6, B3) Elina has a great range of elegant and fun dresses and evening wear in fabulous fabrics, colours and original designs, with matching handbags and accessories. Also stocks a small range of European and Greek designers.
☎ 210 363 1731
✉ Iraklitou 13, Kolonaki
Ⓜ Evangelismos; Syntagma

LAK – Lakis Gavalas (6, B3) The man behind a popular Greek designer boutique has launched his own range and store called LAK, with women's and men's day wear and accessories with a hip edge.
☎ 210 628 3260
✉ Skoufa 10, Kolonaki
Ⓜ Syntagma

CLOTHING & SHOE SIZES

Women's Clothing

Aust/UK	8	10	12	14	16	18
Europe	36	38	40	42	44	46
Japan	5	7	9	11	13	15
USA	6	8	10	12	14	16

Women's Shoes

Aust/USA	5	6	7	8	9	10
Europe	35	36	37	38	39	40
France only	35	36	38	39	40	42
Japan	22	23	24	25	26	27
UK	3½	4½	5½	6½	7½	8½

Men's Clothing

Aust	92	96	100	104	108	112
Europe	46	48	50	52	54	56

Japan	S	M	M		L	
UK/USA	35	36	37	38	39	40

Men's Shirts (Collar Sizes)

Aust/Japan	38	39	40	41	42	43
Europe	38	39	40	41	42	43
UK/USA	15	15½	16	16½	17	17½

Men's Shoes

Aust/ UK	7	8	9	10	11	12
Europe	41	42	43	44½	46	47
Japan	26	27	27.5	28	29	30
USA	7½	8½	9½	10½	11½	12½

*Measurements approximate only;
try before you buy.*

**Yiorgos Eleftheriades
(6, B3)** Trained in costume design, Eleftheriades is known for his edgy alternative classicist, high-design, hand-finished clothes for men and women, using natural fabrics.
☎ 210 361 5278
✉ Pindarou 38, Kolonaki
Ⓜ Evangelismos

INTERNATIONAL DESIGNERS
Carouzos (6, B3) Stocks a huge range of quality, stylish designs by leading men's and women's labels, including Versace, Ferragamo, Fendi, Zegna and Donna Karan. It also stocks a selection of Prada bags and other big-name accessories.
☎ 210 724 5873
✉ Patriarhou Ioakeim 14, Kolonaki
Ⓜ Evangelismos

Central Prince Oliver (6, B3) A three-floor boutique with in-fashion statements from the stars of the international scene, such as Kenzo, Helmut Lang, Etro, Issey Miyake, Paul & Joe, Anna Sui and Yohji Yamamoto.
☎ 210 364 5401
✉ Anagnostopoulou 3, Kolonaki
Ⓜ Evangelismos

Luisa (6, B3) Fashionistas and dreamers will love the A-list of international designers at this super-chic store, including Emilio Pucci, Roberto Cavalli, Gaultier, Missoni and Chloe.
☎ 210 363 5600
✉ Skoufa 17, Kolonaki
Ⓜ Syntagma

Breaking the Fashion Barrier

The fashion-conscious Greeks have always had a strong local market, but the current generation of young designers is starting to make an impact on the international scene.

Leading designers such as Sophia Kokosalaki, Celia Kritharioti and Angelos Frentzos are cutting it on the catwalks and in the fashion houses of Europe and beyond. Other local designers to look out for include Markellos Nihtas, Ioannis Guia, Deux Hommes, Haris & Agelos, Lena Katsanidou, Christoforos Kotentos and Vasso Consola.

Find the latest fashion at Sotris

Sotris (6, B2) Three levels showcasing the latest fashion everything, from clothing to accessories by D&G, Miu Miu, Prada, Venetta Bottega and local success story Angelos Frentzos.
☎ 210 361 0662
✉ Voukourestiou 41 (cnr Tsakalof), Kolonaki
Ⓜ Syntagma

MAINSTREAM FASHION
Artisti Italiani (7, C5) This local fashion chain offers quality and fashionable takes on classic looks, as well as trendy designs in both men's and women's clothing, for day and evening. Look out for the great sales.
☎ 210 331 3857
✉ Ermou 22, Syntagma
Ⓜ Syntagma

Closet (8, E2) A trendy newcomer to the Athens fashion scene, with packed racks of interesting clothes and accessories imported from London,

Italy, Spain and Japan, along with unique pieces from up-and-coming local designers.
☎ 210 331 8526
✉ Sarri 28, Psiri
🕐 noon-3pm & 5-9pm Tue-Fri, 11am-5pm Sat, 3-9pm Sun
Ⓜ Monastiraki

Cop Copine (6, B2) For a contemporary look without a fashion victim tag, this French clothing range has some quality, stylish offerings with an edge.
☎ 210 362 7205
✉ Anagnostopoulou 26-28, Kolonaki
Ⓜ Evangelismos

Epidemic (8, E2) A funky gallery-like store with designer street wear, club wear and accessories with attitude for men and women. Epidemic also sells CDs and designer hair products (and there's a cool hair salon upstairs).
☎ 210 321 1390

✉ Ag Anargyron 16, Psiri
🕐 10am-8pm
Ⓜ Monastiraki

Glou (7, C5) Smart, affordable menswear, including casual and business suits and shirts, as well as mainstream sportswear and accessories.
☎ 210 322 7575
✉ Ermou 49, Syntagma
Ⓜ Syntagma

Zara International (7, C5) This Spanish export has the most affordable fashion in Athens, thus the regular pandemonium, especially on Saturdays – better to go early or on weekdays. Stocks a wide range of womens- and menswear, accessories and kid's wear.
☎ 210 324 9930
✉ Ermou 47, Syntagma
Ⓜ Syntagma

Artisti Italiani; Greek or Italian, great clothes

JEWELLERY & ACCESSORIES

Alexi Andriotti Accessories (7, C5) This Greek franchise is giving growing UK rival Accessorize a run for its money, with stores sprouting all over Athens. An extensive range of costume jewellery, bags and accessories to add colour and flair to your wardrobe.
☎ 210 322 5743
🖳 www.andriotti.com

✉ Ermou 55 & Kapnikareas, Athens Ⓜ Syntagma

Apriati (9, E1) Fun, interesting and affordable handmade pieces from Athena Axioti and other local jewellers, including some unique animal and nature motif designs. Also stocks select prints and ceramics from artists around Greece.

☎ 210 322 9020
🖳 www.apriati.com
✉ Mitropoleos & Pendelis 9, Syntagma
Ⓜ Syntagma

✗ NO!
Archipelagos (9, D3) Unique pieces made from silver and gold for jewellery lovers with more moderate budgets. There are also interesting ceramics and trinkets, including fine silver bookmarks.
☎ 210 323 1321
✉ Adrianou 142 (cnr Thespidos), Plaka
🕑 10am-9pm (later in summer) Ⓜ Monastiraki

Byzantino (9, D2) ✓ Reputedly one of the best of the myriad stores in Plaka selling gold in ancient and Byzantine motifs, the jewellery here is handcrafted by the owners, which means prices are very competitive.
☎ 210 324 6605
✉ Adrianou 120, Plaka
Ⓜ Monastiraki

Demetriadis Art Wear (6, B3) A delectable selection of high-fashion bags, including exclusive designer ranges from Gaultier, Lollypop and XX1, as well as designer jewellery and their own bijoux.
☎ 210 322 7329
✉ Solonos 15, Kolonaki
Ⓜ Syntagma

Elena Votsi (6, B3) Votsi's refreshingly original work, bold designs using exquisite semiprecious stones, sells in New York and London. Her stellar career was boosted

Jewels in Athena's Gown

Gold is not actually produced in Greece – all of it is currently imported. But the quality of workmanship gleaned from a 3000-year-old tradition – and the competition that comes from having thousands of gold- and silversmiths – makes handcrafted Greek jewellery a great buy.

Along with a revival of interest in traditional designs and techniques for making exquisite gold and silver jewellery, artists have recently turned to the craft, making this one of Greece's most thriving and creative industries.

The big names in Greek jewellery, Lalaounis and Zolotas, have promoted Greek jewellery worldwide, as are new generation jewellers such as Elena Votsi, who designed the new Olympic medal. Lalaounis is the only jeweller recognised by the French Academy of Fine Arts and his impressive jewellery museum is worth a visit (see p29).

NEIL SETCHFIELD

Jewellery worthy of a Byzantine emperor at Byzantino

when she was chosen to design the new medal for the Olympics.
☎ 210 360 0936
✉ Xanthou 7, Kolonaki
Ⓜ Evangelismos

Fanourakis (6, B3) Delicate pieces of folded gold characterise Fanourakis' bows, insects and other unique creations. The distinctive designs are sheer art, a factor that is also reflected in the prices. There is also a shop at Panagitsas 6, Kifissia.
☎ 210 721 1762
✉ Patriarhou Ioakeim 23, Kolonaki
Ⓜ Syntagma

Folie-Follie (9, D1) A Greek success story, which has gone global since it started in 1986, you're bound to see these stores around Athens. There's a wide range of watches, bijoux jewellery, shawls, silk and leather bags and other accessories.
☎ 210 323 0601
✉ Ermou 37, Syntagma
Ⓜ Syntagma

Ilias Lalaounis (6, A3) Lalaounis' exquisitely crafted, original creations are considered works of

art, displaying new takes on ancient Greek motifs and inspiration from other cultures, biology, nature and mythology. Lalaounis sells in top jewellery houses around the world.
☎ 210 361 1371
✉ Panepistimiou 6 (cnr Voukourestiou), Kolonaki
Ⓜ Syntagma

Mad Hat (6, B3) Brimming with colour and character, this Greek brand has head wear of every style and finish, from casual straw beach hats to imaginative felt creations, along with bags, belts and accessories also sold in select stores around town.
☎ 210 338 7343
✉ Skoufa 23, Kolonaki
Ⓜ Syntagma

Metalo (9, E1) This tiny corner store carries its own designs in silver and gold, using semiprecious stones and pearls to create interesting, affordable jewellery. There are lovely worry beads and other delectable pieces.
☎ 210 322 7579
✉ Mitropoleos 11, Syntagma Ⓜ Syntagma

Pentheroudakis (6, A3) An established and exclusive Athens jewellery house, Pentheroudakis has modern and simple timeless pieces in precious metals and gemstones. There's also an exclusive array of high-end decorative gifts.
☎ 210 361 3187
✉ Voukourestiou 19 (cnr Valaoritou), Kolonaki
Ⓜ Syntagma

Petai Petai (6, B2) Small individual cabinets contain an eclectic collection of designs, from casual silver pieces to handcrafted gold with precious stones. Owner Ioanna Kokoloupoulou presents her own creations and work from leading local designers.
☎ 210 362 4315
✉ Skoufa 30, Kolonaki
Ⓜ Syntagma

Petridis (6, C3) A gallery-style store with interesting collections from Marianna Petridis and other contemporary Greek jewellers such as Katerina Anesti and Doretta Tonti. A good choice for elegant, handmade, original designs.
☎ 210 721 7789
✉ Haritos 34, Kolonaki
Ⓜ Evangelismos

Zolotas (7, D5) Internationally renowned jeweller Zolotas breathes life into ancient Greece with replicas of museum pieces. Since 1972, the company has had the exclusive rights to make exact copies of the real thing.
☎ 210 331 3320
✉ Stadiou 9, Syntagma
Ⓜ Syntagma

SHOES & LEATHER GOODS

Bournazos (9, E1) These Greek designs for men and women have gained international recognition for their quality, workmanship and style. Bournazos also has a good range of bags and leather accessories, and stores throughout Athens.
☎ 210 325 5580
✉ Ermou 15, Syntagma
Ⓜ Syntagma

Charalas (9, D1) This popular Ermou option has a wide selection of quality leather shoes and bags, from the latest out-there fashions to Nine West classics.
☎ 210 325 8100
✉ Ermou 30, Syntagma
Ⓜ Syntagma

Danos (6, B3) Artful window displays showcase Danos' feminine, individual designs, made in Greece from the finest imported leathers.

There is also a select range of international designs.
☎ 210 362 5390
✉ Filikis Eterias Sq 6, Kolonaki Ⓜ Evangelismos

Fontana (7, C4) Housed in a grand old arcade lined with similar stores, Fontana carries a fine range of Italian, French and Greek leather diaries, wallets, briefcases, accessories and travel goods.
☎ 210 323 2093
✉ Arsakiou Arcade 3 (off Panepistimiou), Athens
Ⓜ Panepistimio

Kalogirou (6, B3) Shoe fetishists will love the offerings in colours and styles to blow the imagination and budget, with top international designers, as well as Kologirou's own creations. Avoid the Saturday morning rush by the boutique set.
☎ 210 722 8804

✉ Patriarhou Ioakeim 4, Kolonaki Ⓜ Evangelismos

Kem (6, B3) A popular Greek brand with an excellent range of stylish leather bags for the working woman, in durable modern and classic designs.
☎ 210 721 9230 ✉ Patriarhou Ioakeim 26a, Kolonaki Ⓜ Evangelismos

Prasini (6, B3) Imelda Marcos would have gone nuts in this shoe heaven, with French, Italian, Spanish and Greek designer footwear for the really well-heeled, indeed. Not to mention the bags.
☎ 210 364 1590
✉ Tsakalof 7-9, Kolonaki
Ⓜ Evangelismos

Spiliopoulos (9, C1) It is usually chaos, but there are bargains among the over-crowded racks of imported shoes and bags from top brands such as La Spiga and Kate Spade, usually at wholesale prices. It also stocks leather jackets, and there's a second store on Adrianou.
☎ 210 322 7590
✉ Ermou 63, Athens
Ⓜ Syntagma

Stavros' Sandals

He's known locally as the poet sandal maker, and septuagenarian **Stavros Melissinos' store** (8, F3; ☎ 210 321 9247; Pandrosou 89; Ⓜ Monastiraki) is the place to get that pair of traditional Jesus sandals, lace-up Roman ones or fancy sequined leather variations on the theme.

For poems or sandals, Stavros is the man to see

Thiros (6, B3) An established Greek label with well-priced leather bags in classic and contemporary designs. Everything from tiny evening purses to work and weekend bags.
☎ 210 362 8445
✉ Pindarou 21 (cnr Skoufa), Kolonaki
Ⓜ Syntagma

ART & ANTIQUES

Antiqua (9, F1) Serious Greek and European antiques from the 15th to 19th centuries, with a good selection of silverware, clocks, paintings and icons. Expect to pay accordingly.
☎ 210 323 2220
✉ Amalias 2-4, Syntagma
Ⓜ Syntagma

Antiquarius (6, B3) A well-established specialist in imported antiques and collectables, mostly from the UK and France. Items include books, prints, silver, crystal, embroideries and small furniture pieces.
☎ 210 360 6454
✉ Anagnostopoulou 8, Kolonaki Ⓜ Syntagma

Athena Gallerie (9, D1) This gallery and restaurant in Plaka has a large range of paintings, silk-screen prints and lithographs by leading Greek artists, and an exhibition space for guest artists.
☎ 210 331 5209
✉ Mnisikleous 7b, Plaka
🕑 9am-2am
Ⓜ Monastiraki

Dexippos Art Gallery (9, C1) Most of the pieces here are commissioned from a group of skilled artists producing museum copies and original designs influenced by ancient Greece, including sculptures, frescoes, paintings and ceramics.
☎ 210 324 7688 ✉ Dexippou 1 (cnr Panos), Plaka
Ⓜ Monastiraki

Martinos (8, F3) This Plaka landmark opened in 1890 and still has a great selection of Greek and European antiques, including painted dowry chests, icons, coins, glassware, porcelain and furniture.
☎ 210 321 2414
🖥 www.martinosart.gr
✉ Pandrosou 50, Monastiraki Ⓜ Monastiraki

Michael Mihalakos (6, A2) A good place to hunt for collectables such as china, prints, paintings, glassware, silver, fancy light fittings and bigger furniture items.
☎ 210 362 6182
✉ Solonos 32, Kolonaki
Ⓜ Syntagma

Moraitis (9, D3) Takis Moraitis lives and works in his studio-gallery, where you will find his trademark island landscapes and often the artist and his students at work. A café was in the works in the great lower-level gallery, with a huge fireplace.
☎ 210 322 5208 ✉ Adrianou 129, Plaka 🕑 11am-11pm Ⓜ Akropoli

✴ CLOSED/VACATION
Paleopolion o Alexandros (8, E3) This landmark store on Thisiou is bursting with collectables, crockery, amber worry beads, postcards and memorabilia such as commemorative plates featuring Greek royalty.
☎ 210 321 2414 ✉ Thisiou 10, Monastiraki
Ⓜ Thisio

Skoufa Gallery (6, B3) As well as regular exhibitions from local artists, the gallery

Will this fit in my suitcase? Skoufa Gallery

has sculptures, paintings, prints and a select collection of small antique pieces and interesting *objets d'art*.
☎ 210 360 3541
✉ Skoufa 4, Kolonaki
Ⓜ Evangelismos

Stavros Mihalarias (6, B3) The art and antiques here are strictly for hard-core collectors, but the restored Kolonaki stately mansion is worth wandering through. Mihalarias is a world-renowned expert in the restoration of icons and fine art and holds art auctions annually.
☎ 210 721 0689
✉ Alopekis (cnr Irodotou), Kolonaki
Ⓜ Evangelismos

Zoumboulakis Gallery (6, A3) Stocks an excellent range of limited edition prints and posters by leading Greek artists, including Tsarouhis, Mytara and Fassianos. Zoumboulakis also sells art and antiques at the Kolonaki store (Haritos 26) for top-end collectors.
☎ 210 363 4454
✉ Kriezotou 7, Syntagma
Ⓜ Syntagma

CRAFTS, GIFTS & SOUVENIRS

Aidini (9, E2) Errikos Aidini is an artisan with metal, with work in leading galleries. You may catch him at his craft in his workshop at the back of this store. Well-priced original creations include small mirrors, candlesticks, boats, planes and his signature bronze daisies.
☎ 210 323 4591
✉ Nikis 32, Plaka
Ⓜ Syntagma

Amorgos (9, E2) A charming store crammed with authentic Greek folk art, trinkets, ceramics, embroideries and collectables, plus wood-carved furniture and items made by owner Kostas Kaitatzis, whose wife Rena runs the store.
☎ 210 324 3836
✉ Kodrou 3, Plaka
🕑 11am-3pm & 6-8pm Mon-Fri Ⓜ Syntagma

Benaki Museum Gift Shop (6, B3) Some of the best replicas of Greek artefacts, jewellery, prints and books are sold here, as well as an exquisite collection of icons, from reasonably priced copies to pieces worth a small fortune.
☎ 210 362 7367
✉ Koumbari 1, Kolonaki
Ⓜ Evangelismos

Centre of Hellenic Tradition (8, F3) ✓ Upstairs in this arcade are great examples of traditional ceramics, sculptures, woodcarvings, paintings and folk art from prominent Greek artists. The cute café/ouzeri has Acropolis views, and there's also a gallery upstairs.
☎ 210 321 3023
✉ Pandrosou 36 (or Mitropoleos 59), Monastiraki 🕑 9am-8pm (winter 9am-7pm)
Ⓜ Monastiraki

Eommex (9, E1) A huge showroom run by a traditional cooperative selling handmade rugs made by more than 30 weavers around the country.
☎ 210 323 0408
✉ Mitropoleos 9, Syntagma Ⓜ Syntagma

Fancy a Flokati?

There are endless possibilities for souvenirs, from small items such as worry beads, traditional fishermen's hats, charms and Greek sea sponges to high-end museum copies of ancient Greek art.

Plaka and Monastiraki are lined with stores selling *tavli* (backgammon) sets (below), colourful hand-blown glass, hanging oil lamps, Byzantine icons, hand-painted ceramics, handicrafts such as olive-wood key rings, flokati (woollen rugs) and other hand-woven rugs. There is also a huge selection of handcrafted silver and gold jewellery, art and modern sculpture in ceramic, bronze and marble.

Olive Wood sells handmade items of olive wood, a perfect gift for olive lovers

Georgiadis (7, B4) A traditional store in the busy Central Market area selling classic Greek tin kitchen accessories, from brightly coloured wine decanters to stainless steel olive oil pourers, trays, lanterns and even intricate wire mousetraps.
☎ 210 321 2193
✉ Sofokleous 35, Omonia ⏲ 7am-3pm Mon-Sat Ⓜ Omonia

Keramar (1, B2) A huge selection of pottery and ceramics from 170 workshops all over Greece, including hand-painted traditional ceramics, jugs and pots. It's a bit of a hike but it's a good place to go for pottery or a giant urn to ship home.
☎ 210 802 5332 ✉ Kifissias 207, Maroussi ⏲ 9am-9pm 🚌 550 **(get off at Ageioplastiki stop)**

Koukos (9, E2) This store has a wonderful collection of Italian pewter picture frames, platters, jugs,

replicas of old monk's hip flasks and other items. Koukos also stocks a range of antique ceramics and original silver handcrafted jewellery.
☎ 210 322 2740
✉ Navarhou Nikodimou 21, Plaka Ⓜ Syntagma

Museum of Cycladic Art Shop (6, B3) There are many treasures to be found in this impressive gift shop, including exclusive Cycladic figurines and pottery (copied or inspired from the museum's collection) and beautiful books on ancient Greek art.
☎ 210 724 9706
✉ Neofytou Douka 4, Kolonaki ⏲ 10am-4pm Mon, Wed-Fri, 10am-3pm Sat Ⓜ Evangelismos

Mythos (9, E2) This narrow store at the fringes of Plaka's tourist drag has a fine selection of interesting and reasonably priced jewellery, artwork, crafts and other goodies that make great small gifts. Worth a peek.
☎ 210 324 9160

✉ Kydathineon 6, Plaka ⏲ 10am-10.30pm (winter 10am-9pm) Ⓜ Syntagma

National Welfare Organisation (9, D1) Traditional folk art and crafts from all over Greece, including stunning hand-woven carpets, kilims, flokati rugs, tapestries, hand-embroidered table-cloths, cushion covers and ceramics.
☎ 210 321 8272
✉ Ipatias 6 (cnr Apollonos), Plaka Ⓜ Syntagma

Olive Wood (9, D1) Original creations from half a dozen families in Greece who work exclusively with wood from olive trees – a wood which is so hard it can only be carved, not nailed. The shop has everything, from ornaments to wooden spoons, key rings and chopping blocks (apparently ideal as the timber is scratch resistant).
☎ 210 321 6145
✉ Mnisikleous 8, Plaka Ⓜ Syntagma

MUSIC & BOOKS

Compendium (9, E2) A good selection of new and used books, with popular and quality literature, travel guides, books on Greece and academic publications.
☎ 210 322 1248
✉ Nikis 28, Plaka
Ⓜ Syntagma

Eleftheroudakis (6, A3) A seven-storey bibliophile's paradise with the widest selection of books from and on Greece, plus English-language books, including maps and travel guides. The excellent café on the top floor is run by the Food Company (p73). There's also a branch at Nikis 20, Plaka.
☎ 210 331 4180 ✉ Pan-epistimiou 17, Syntagma
☾ 9am-9pm Mon-Fri, 9am-3pm Sat Ⓜ Syn-tagma; Panepistimio

Metropolis (7, C3) A music haven well stocked with local and international CDs, with extensive specialist

sections such as dance/hip-hop and progressive rock/postelectronica. The alphabetical listings are a little confusing. A bigger Greek selection is in the dedicated store further along Panepistimiou.
☎ 210 383 0804
✉ Panepistimiou 64, Omonia ☾ 9am-9pm Mon-Fri, 9am-6pm Sat Ⓜ Omonia

Nasiotis (8, F3) There are literally stacks of old first editions, rare books, magazines and engravings along the arcade and in the packed basement, as well as old Greek movie and advertising posters and postcards.
☎ 210 321 2369
✉ Ifestou 24, Monasti-raki Ⓜ Monastiraki

Pandora Music Shop (6, A1) The place to go for that bouzouki or other beautifully hand-crafted traditional Greek instru-

Pick up a new skill at Pandora Music Shop

ments, such as the *baglama* (a mini-bouzouki), lutes and tambourines.
☎ 210 361 9924
✉ Mavromihali 51, Ex-arhia ☾ 11am-3pm Mon, Wed & Sat, 11am-2pm & 5.30-8pm Tue, Thu & Fri Ⓜ Panepistimio

Tzina (7, C3) This compact, cramped little store has a good variety of well-categorised music, with some bargains, interesting oddities and best-ofs to be found. One level is dedicated to Greek music, the other to the rest of the spectrum.
☎ 210 325 1271
✉ Panepistimiou 57, Omonia Ⓜ Omonia

Virgin Megastore (7, D5) There are plenty of headsets at Virgin to listen to the latest releases and a wide selection of Greek CDs and every other sort of music, as well as video games, PlayStations and other toys for big kids.
☎ 210 331 4788
✉ Stadiou 7-9, Syn-tagma ☾ 9am-9pm Mon-Fri, 9am-6pm Sat Ⓜ Syntagma

Zorba & More

Plenty of dreamy books have been written about Greece and the Greek islands but not many touch exclusively on Athens.

Henry Miller was inspired by the city's light and rhythm in the 1950s and his classic novel *The Colossus of Maroussi* is still a good, if rather pompous, read. *Dinner with Persephone* is the result of American Patricia Storace's year living in Athens. Andreas Staikos' *Les Liaisons Culinaires* is a mouth-watering erotic account of an Athens love triangle where the men seduce with food (complete with recipes). But for a taste of the essence of Greece, you can't beat the classic *Zorba the Greek*, by Nikos Kazantzakis.

FOOD & DRINK

Aristokratikon (7, D5)
Chocaholics will be delighted by the dazzling array of freshly handmade chocolates at this tiny store renowned for using the finest ingredients in Greece. If you're in need of a choccie while in Kifissia, there's another store at Argyropoulou 8 (3, B1; ☎ 210 801 6533). Not one for the weak-willed. Try the pistachio clusters.
☎ 210 322 0546
✉ **Karageorgi Servias 9, Syntagma** Ⓜ **Syntagma**

Cellier (7, D5) A wonderful collection of some of Greece's best wines and liqueurs, with knowledgeable staff to explain the Greek varieties and winemakers. It also sells boxed gift packs. Also Papadiemanti 10, Kifissia (3, B1; ☎ 210 801 8756).
☎ 210 361 0040
✉ **Kriezotou 1, Syntagma**
Ⓜ **Syntagma**

Golden Booths

The *periptero*, the ubiquitous small yellow kiosk, is a quintessentially Greek institution and the best place to call for anything from directions, cigarettes, bus tickets and newspapers to condoms and light bulbs. The ones around Syntagma and Omonia are open 24 hours.

Karavan (7, E4) A tiny store with rows of sweets and delicious, honey-soaked, nut-filled variations of baklava, including bite-sized, low-guilt versions for a harmless treat.
☎ 210 364 1540
✉ **Voukourestiou 11, Kolonaki** Ⓜ **Syntagma**

Fine Wine (9, D3) A great selection of fine Greek wines and spirits, including gift packs, in a delightful, refurbished old Plaka store. The friendly and knowledgeable staff can guide you through Greece's unique

grape varieties.
☎ 210 323 0350
✉ **Lysikratous 3, Plaka**
🕒 10am-10pm Mon-Fri, 10am-8pm Sat
Ⓜ **Syntagma**

Mesogaia (9, E2) An excellent range of traditional food products from all over Greece, including cheeses, yogurts and biscuits for immediate consumption or take-home jars of thyme honey with walnuts, *pasteli* (honey and sesame sweets) from Andros, sweets, olives, olive oil and other delectable products.
☎ 210 322 9146
✉ **Nikis 52 (cnr Kydathineon), Plaka**
🕒 9am-5pm Mon & Wed, 9am-9pm Tue, Thu & Fri, 9am-4pm Sat, plus in winter only 10am-3pm Sun Ⓜ **Syntagma**

Miseyiannis (6, B3) A wonderful selection of Greek coffee (and any other type you can imagine), with all the necessary accessories such as a brass *briki* (Greek coffee maker) and special coffee cups.
☎ 210 721 0136
✉ **Leventi 7, Kolonaki**
Ⓜ **Evangelismos**

Mesogaia's hampers take picnics to a whole new level

NEIL SETCHFIELD

FOR CHILDREN

Baby Natura (6, B3)
Exquisite clothing and accessories for newborns and young infants, with special christening outfits, bed linen, shoes, toys, nursery decorations and body products – even amulets to guard against the evil eye.
☎ 210 361 5494
✉ **Milioni 10, Kolonaki**
Ⓜ **Syntagma**

Crocodilino (9, E1) The shoe fetish in Greece starts at an early age so the selection of kid's shoes is excellent. The extensive range at Crocodilino is Italian made.
☎ 210 324 4662
✉ **Voulis 24, Syntagma**
Ⓜ **Syntagma**

Gelato (9, D1) Good-quality, fashionable children's wear for newborns and children up to 12 years old. Most of the clothing is made in Greece and is well priced.
☎ 210 322 1777
✉ **Ermou 48, Athens**
Ⓜ **Syntagma**

You're never too young for good footwear at Crocodilino

Lapin House (9, E1)
This children's wear store, opened by a group of Greeks nearly 30 years ago, now has branches in Australia, Italy, the Middle East and New York. Excellent quality, stylish gear for kids of all ages.
☎ 210 324 1316
✉ **Ermou 21, Syntagma**
Ⓜ **Syntagma**

Mauve (6, B2) A unique boutique with old-world charm, Mauve has *haute couture* baby wear, baptismal outfits, bonnets, bibs and sheet sets in lace, lush drapes and a superb selection of antique fabrics.

☎ 210 364 0142
✉ **Dimokritou 24 (cnr An-agnostopoulou), Kolonaki**
🕐 **closed Aug** Ⓜ **Evangelismos; Syntagma**

Parthenis (6, B2) The children's wear range of this established Greek designer, known for quality casual sportswear, has simple monochrome comfortable clothing in fine linens, cottons (and velour in winter) and other natural fabrics.
☎ 210 363 3158
✉ **Dimokritou 20 (cnr Tsakalof), Kolonaki**
Ⓜ **Evangelismos**

Beware the Evil Eye

The evil eye is associated with envy, and can be cast – apparently unintentionally – upon someone or something which is praised, coveted or admired (even secretly).

Most culprits are those who are considered peculiar in some way by the locals. Folk with blue eyes are also suspicious; all they have to do is be present when someone or something enviable appears on the scene – and then the trouble starts.

Protection from the evil eye comes from wearing blue or keeping a blue-glass talisman (usually in the shape of an eye) close by. This is a welcome alternative for children or babies (considered especially vulnerable), whose mothers pretend to spit on them to deflect any ill effects.

SPECIALIST STORES

Baba (9, B1) This little hole in the wall has been around for ages, selling a small but good range of backgammon sets – a favourite Greek pastime – in all sizes. The best are handmade with inlaid wood.
☎ 210 321 9994
✉ Ifestou 30, Monastiraki Ⓜ Monastiraki

Filokalia (9, E1) All manner of ecclesiastical paraphernalia is sold here, including icons, incense, candles and *tamata* (votive offerings), as well as books on the Greek Orthodox faith.
☎ 210 323 4411
✉ Voulis 38, Plaka Ⓜ Syntagma

Kamarinos (7, C5) Kamarinos stocks exquisite antiquarian maps, some dating back to 1500, as well as more than 10,000 faithful reproduction prints from old books and periodicals.
☎ 210 323 0923
✉ Kolokotroni 15a, Syntagma Ⓜ Syntagma

Kaplan Furs (9, E1) The best furs in Greece are made in the northern city of Kastoria, although the once-thriving industry has suffered from the anti-fur campaigns that have made them most un-PC. Kaplan has a huge selection in various styles.
☎ 210 322 2226
✉ Mitropoleos 22-24, Syntagma Ⓜ Syntagma

Korres (7, E7) You can get the full range from local natural beauty product guru George Korres at his only retail store – at a fraction of the price you'll pay in London or New York. The excellent hair and skin care products are also available in most good pharmacies around Athens.
☎ 210 756 0600
🖳 www.korres.com
✉ Ivikou 8, Pangrati (near Panathenaic stadium) 🚌 2, 4, 11

Mazarakis (9, E1) A huge selection of kilims, carpets, rugs and luxurious traditional Greek flokati rugs that can be packed into surprisingly small parcels to take home – or staff can have them shipped back for you.
☎ 210 323 9428
✉ Voulis 31-33, Syntagma Ⓜ Syntagma

Pylarinos (7, D5) An undisputed authority on Greek coins and publisher of the definitive Greek numismatics guide spanning 250 years, Pylarinos has stamps dating back to 1828.
☎ 210 363 0688
✉ Panepistimiou 18 (in arcade), Syntagma Ⓜ Syntagma

Vraki (6, A2) This quirky store is as close as you get to a men's lingerie store, with an extensive range of funky underwear and T-shirt ensembles from the Thessaloniki-based designer. There's a smaller women's range and unisex designs.
☎ 210 362 7420
✉ Skoufa 50, Kolonaki Ⓜ Syntagma

Mystic Mastic

Since ancient times, scientists have recognised the unique medicinal benefits of mastic, the resin from the mastic trees that mysteriously grow only on the island of Chios.

Mastic Spa (7, E5; ☎ 210 360 3413; www.unique-mastic.com; Iraklitou 1, Kolonaki) has a sophisticated range of skin and hair products, toothpaste, gum, perfumes and candles made from mastic and Chios herbs.

Mastiha Shop (7, D5; ☎ 210 363 2750; www.mastihashop.com; Panepistimiou 6, Syntagma; ⏰ 9am-9pm) is an initiative of the Mastic Growers Association of Chios and sells mastic-based food products, as well as pharmaceuticals, cosmetics, essential oils and other Chios products.

Eating

Eating out is a key part of Athenian culture, as the plethora of restaurants around town confirms. Fresh local produce, the diversity of regional specialities and creative new takes on traditional dishes offer plenty of delights. A boom in the Athens culinary scene has seen a proliferation of new restaurants and cafés and a trend towards other ethnic cuisines.

There are options for all palates (and budgets), from tasty lamb chops and salad at neighbourhood tavernas to fancy French restaurants and sushi (a recent craze, but few places have mastered the art).

Old-style casual neighbourhood tavernas remain one of the simple pleasures, and Greeks can do wonders with fish. However, Greek cuisine is becoming more sophisticated and the past decade has seen the emergence of upmarket *nuevo*-tavernas, taking traditional flavours and dishes to a new level (and too often the prices as well).

Many restaurants are also bars, which means things liven up after midnight. Most of the restaurants around Plaka and the Acropolis cater to the tourist market, serving standard taverna fare and predictable favourites. The more contemporary and trendy restaurants in the city centre are in Psiri, Kolonaki and Gazi, but it's worth venturing out to the waterfront at Piraeus or from Glyfada to Vouliagmeni, or north to Kifissia.

Athens has a distinct seasonal dining culture, which means many of the best restaurants will close for the summer, often moving to sister restaurants on the islands. In summer it is all alfresco dining, while winter is an entirely different indoor experience.

Meal Costs

The pricing symbols used in this chapter indicate the cost for one person having a two-course meal, excluding drinks.

$	€15 and under
$$	€16-25
$$$	€26-39
$$$$	over €40

Dining Hours

The first thing you should know about the Athens restaurant scene is that Greeks eat late. Average dinner bookings are at 10pm and it is not uncommon for tables to start filling at midnight. Some of the best restaurants in town don't open until 9pm, so if you want some atmosphere don't arrive early.

More tourist-friendly eateries open earlier, but if you want to do as the Athenians do, have a late lunch and maybe even sneak in a siesta so you can enjoy things in full swing later on, especially in summer. Reservations are highly recommended for the more up-market restaurants.

ACROPOLIS & THISIO

Dionyssos-Zonar's (9, B3) $$$
Greek/International
A tourist favourite directly opposite the Acropolis, Dionyssos has extensive outdoor seating and a broad menu. It is also home to Zonar's Cafe, the former Athenian landmark forced to move in 2000. Expect to pay top dollar for the view.
☎ 210 922 1998
✉ Rovertou Galli 43, Makrigianni ⏰ lunch & dinner; café breakfast & lunch Ⓜ Akropoli

Filistron (9, A2) $$
Mezedopolio
A rooftop terrace with Acropolis views makes this a pleasant place for dinner on a summer night; the food won't disappoint either. Offerings include a simple, tasty range of mezedhes such as grilled cheese, village-style sausage and meatballs, and a good selection of greens and salads.
☎ 210 346 7554
✉ Apostolou Pavlou 23, Thisio ⏰ dinner, lunch summer & Sun Ⓜ Thisio

Pil Poul (8, D3) $$$$
Mediterranean/International
For fine dining, ambience and a million-dollar view, Pil Poul's rooftop terrace is unsurpassed. This classy 1920s neoclassical mansion, frequented by wealthy locals and foreign dignitaries, has a modern Mediterranean menu with strong French influences. Dress up and book ahead.
☎ 210 342 3665

Great Views

For the ultimate romantic evening with views of the illuminated Acropolis, you can't beat **Pil Poul** (pictured below), or the informal alternative, **Strofi** (below). High-end newcomer **Orizontes** on Lykavittos (p73) takes in the whole panorama. For a seaside dinner, head to **Istioploikos** (p90) in Piraeus, where you can dine (or just have a drink) on a huge boat-turned-restaurant overlooking Mikrolimano harbour. Or take in the city from the rooftop bar of the **Grand Bretagne** (p96) or the Hilton's **Galaxy Bar** (p96).

✉ Apostolou Pavlou 51 (cnr Poulopoulou), Thisio ⏰ dinner Mon-Sat Ⓜ Thisio

Strofi (7, B7) $$
Taverna
This charming taverna has a rooftop terrace with superb Acropolis views and is a regular hang-out of the theatre set after performances at the nearby Theatre of Herodes Atticus. Glossy photos on the walls downstairs are testament to its many famous guests. Strofi serves a standard array of quality taverna classics at affordable prices.
☎ 210 921 4130
✉ Rovertou Galli 25,

Makrigianni ⏰ dinner Mon-Sat Ⓜ Akropoli

To Steki tou Ilia (8, D3) $
Taverna/Psistaria
One of the best places for meat eaters, Ilia's has celebrity status (and clients). Lamb chops are sold by the kilo and grilled to perfection. For variety, there are pork chops and steaks too, as well as dips, chips and salads. In summer, there are tables outside in front of the church.
☎ 210 342 2407
✉ Thessalonikis 7, Thisio ⏰ dinner Tue-Sun, lunch Sun Ⓜ Thisio

EXARHIA

Barba Gianni's (7, D3) $
Taverna
An Exarhia classic, popular with students and those wanting a cheap, hearty meal in a no-frills traditional taverna. There are huge trays of *mageirefta* and simple Greek fare on offer, washed down with cheap wine and lots of atmosphere.
☎ 210 330 0185
✉ E Benaki 94, Exarhia
🕐 lunch & dinner
Ⓜ Omonia ♿

Cookou Food (7, D3) $
Greek/International
A casual, trendy eatery serving great value lunches, with trays of fresh traditional Greek dishes and other specials like spinach lasagne and orange chicken with basmati rice. The unique décor is the work of the artist half of this partnership. There's a slightly more pricey à la carte menu in the evenings.
☎ 210 330 2933
✉ Themistokleous 66, Exarhia 🕐 lunch & dinner Ⓜ Omonia ♿

Taverna Rozalia (7, D3) $
Taverna
An old Exarhia haunt, Rozalia is a family-run taverna with a huge courtyard garden, which recently installed special fans that spray water to keep you cool. Excellent value grilled meats, traditional cooking and house wine ensure it is always lively. In winter go across the street to sister

restaurant, Vergina.
☎ 210 330 2933
✉ Valtetsiou 58, Exarhia 🕐 lunch & dinner
Ⓜ Omonia ♿

Yiantes (7, D3) $$
Modern Greek
Yiantes is a little oasis next to the Riviera open-air cinema, with trees towering over a delightful colourful courtyard, and funky retro décor inside. Creative regional specialities from all over Greece are on offer, with contemporary touches and ample servings. Try the Byzantine pork with coriander.
☎ 210 330 1369
✉ Valtetsiou 44, Exarhia 🕐 lunch & dinner Ⓜ Omonia

Smack Your Lips Around a Souvlaki

Whether it's the meat on a stick variety, *gyros* or the spicy mince kebab-style variation on the theme, the souvlaki is the best quick and cheap meal in town and you can't leave Athens without trying one. The versions you get overseas just don't compare.

Souvlaki heaven is found in Monastiraki at the end of Mitropoleos, where the unmistakable aromas make it hard to resist. It is packed with diners day and night and the live music, compliments of musicians sitting at one of the tables, gives it a festive feel. **Thanasis (9, C1;** ☎ 210 324 4705; Mitropoleos 69; 🕐 8.30am-2.30am) is among the best, with special mince kebab-style meat on pitta.

ALAN BENSON

GAZI & ROUF

Aristera-Dexia (8, A3) $$$
Modern Greek/International
This super-cool converted car workshop is one of the best restaurants in Athens, with exciting takes on Mediterranean flavours and an excellent wine list. Style is at a premium – from the novel video-screen entry to the Campari bottle light fittings, glass cellar and open kitchen bar – even the toilets are a talking point. In summer, a more casual menu is on offer in the courtyard.
☎ 210 342 2380 ✉ Andronikou 3, Rouf (entry from Tzaferi in summer) 🕒 dinner 🚕 taxi

Dirty Str-eat (8, C1) $$
Bar/Restaurant
Modern-style, multi-ethnic cuisine and a cool, artfully decorated courtyard makes this one of Gazi's trendiest eateries, along with sister restaurant Dirty Ginger further down the street.
☎ 210 347 4763
✉ Triptolemou 12, Gazi

Taste food like your mother never made at Mamacas

🕒 dinner, lunch Sun 🚕 taxi

Mamacas (8, B2) $$
Traditional Greek
Decked out in cool pastel shades, this Gazi trailblazer puts a modern touch on traditional dishes (once cooked, as the name implies, by the owners' mothers). Try the daily specials or staples such as the Mykonian sausage or black-eyed bean salad. In summer, outdoor seating sprawls across the street to a newer courtyard addition.
☎ 210 346 4984
✉ Persefonis 41, Gazi

🕒 lunch & dinner Mon-Sat 🚕 taxi

Skoufias (8, A3) $$
Taverna
A delightful taverna serving Cretan-style food and an excellent, eclectic selection of regional Greek cooking, including game and unusual dishes. The tables are spread next to the church across the road. In winter it moves to a charming building in Petralona where there is excellent live acoustic music.
☎ 210 341 2252
✉ Vasiliou Tou Megalou 50, Rouf 🕒 dinner Mon-Sat 🚕 taxi

Thalatta (8, C3) $$$
International
A classy addition to the Gazi scene in a tastefully restored old neoclassical building, Thalatta specialises in seafood, but has other tasty offerings too. The sea theme extends to the décor. There is a fine wine list, some excellent desserts and a lovely courtyard for alfresco dining.
☎ 210 346 4204 ✉ Vitonos 5, Gazi 🕒 dinner Mon-Sat 🚕 taxi

Taverna vs Medezoplio

A *taverna* is more casual and far cheaper than a restaurant *(estiatorio)*, serving traditional Greek fare and often only house wine. Modern tavernas have a fancier version of traditional dishes in a more trendy setting. A *psistaria* specialises in grilled meats, with some basic salads and starters. *Medezopolia* serve a variety of meze (appetiser-sized dishes, bigger than tapas), which is usually shared. An *ouzeri* is similar to a *mezedopolio*, but traditionally ouzo is usually drunk to rinse the palate between tastes (not mandatory of course). *Mageirefta* or *mageiria* refers to casserole-style or oven-baked dishes.

INNER CITY

Edodi (7, B8) $$$
Modern Greek/International
A tantalising 'live' menu, where waiters parade huge platters of the prepared (yet-to-be cooked) dishes of the day, makes for a truly unique dining experience at this stylish, tiny restaurant in an elegant neoclassical building. The food is creative and delicious, with some wicked desserts. A very special night out. Reservations essential.
☎ 210 921 3013 ✉ Veikou 80, Koukaki ⏱ dinner Mon-Sat (closed Aug) Ⓜ Syngrou-Fix

Kallimarmaron (7, E6) $$
Traditional Greek
Regional specialities with an edge, and excellent seasonal dishes using creative ingredients, are complemented by a warm cosy atmosphere in this established restaurant. Old photos hang on the wall from the time the family ran the café at the old Olympic

There's just too much good food at Vlassis

Stadium nearby.
☎ 210 701 9727 ✉ Eforionos 13 (cnr Eratosthenous), Pangrati ⏱ lunch & dinner Mon-Sat 🚌 2, 4 11

Karavitis (7, F6) $
Taverna
A no-frills, prewar taverna with a pleasant garden courtyard that gets busy in summer and a rustic room filled with old barrels for winter. The barrel wine is drinkable and the food cheap and reliable. It has an old-Greece feel and all the taverna favourites: dips, salads, excellent meatballs and grilled meats.
☎ 210 721 5155 ✉ Pafsaniou 4 (cnr Arktinou), Pangrati ⏱ dinner

(garden open May-Oct) Ⓜ Evangelismos (plus walk)

Spondi (7, F8) $$$
Modern Greek/Mediterranean
This Michelin-rated restaurant in a lovely old Athens mansion has a wonderful ambience and superb courtyard for summer dining. Applauded for its imaginative dishes such as tender pork fillets with *myzithra* cheese in a fig and yogurt salsa, the desserts are also considered among the best in Athens. Reservations essential.
☎ 210 756 4021 ✉ Pyrronos 5 (off Plateia Varnava), Pangrati ⏱ dinner 🚖 taxi

Vlassis (6, E1) $$
Taverna
Quality, classic Greek cuisine and a tasteful setting make this one of the best upscale, but modest, tavernas in Athens. An enticing range of starters and favourites such as spinach pie, cabbage *dolmades* and sardines are enough for you to skip the mains and go straight to desserts, such as the halva.
☎ 210 646 3060 ✉ Pasteur 8 , Ambelokipi ⏱ dinner (closed mid-Jul–mid-Sep) Ⓜ Ambelokipi

---

I'll Drink to That!

Good old retsina has its place, but it has unfortunately done a grave disservice to Greek wine, which is finally beginning to raise its head internationally. There are some fine wineries making excellent wines from Greece's unique native grape varieties – reds such as *agiorgitiko* and *xinomavro* and the whites *asyrtiko*, *roditis*, *robola*, *malagouzia* and *moschofilero*.

The industry is becoming more sophisticated as the new generation of winemakers concentrates on producing the best from Greece's climate and varieties. The results are certainly worth a try (see www.greekwineguide.gr).

KOLONAKI

Boschetto (6, C3) $$$$
Modern Italian
In the gardens of Evangel-ismos Park, Boschetto is a relaxed, classy place to eat in summer and a refreshing escape from the bustle of Athens. The *nouvelle* Italian cuisine offers some enticing delights, and pasta is the house speciality. There's an extensive range of vintage Greek and international wines.
☎ 210 721 0893
✉ Vasilissis Sofias, (Evangelismos Park), Kolonaki ☼ dinner Mon-Sat ⓂEvangelismos

Filippou (6, C3) $$
Taverna
Bookings are recommended at this classic taverna in the Dexameni district, which is always packed with locals enjoying the renowned home-cooked fare at prices rare for this neighbourhood. There's a courtyard and tables on the pavement across the road.
☎ 210 721 6390
✉ Xenokratous 19, Kolonaki ☼ lunch & dinner (closed Sat night & Sun) ⓂEvangelismos

Food Company (7, E4) $
Café/Restaurant
Run by a Canadian, this is the only place in town with a range of wholesome ready-made multi-ethnic dishes, including pasta, couscous, curried chicken with rice, Spanish meatballs and delicious roast chicken with rosemary. Great for a casual meal, or get takeaway for a picnic. The cakes are also worth the hike up the hill.
☎ 210 361 6619
✉ Anagnostopoulou 47
☼ 9am-midnight Mon-Sat, noon-midnight Sun
Ⓜ Evangelismos

Il Parmigiano (7, D4) $$
Italian
A variety of *al dente* pasta dishes and classic Italian cuisine make this a popular place for a casual lunch or dinner. It's in a pedestrian cul-de-sac off busy Skoufa.
☎ 210 364 1414 ✉ Gri-veon 3 ☼ lunch & dinner Ⓜ Syntagma

Jackson Hall (7, E5) $$
Bar/Restaurant
This trendy, overpriced three-level bar-cum-restaurant buzzes day and night. American-style burgers and steaks are the speciality, but the seafood pastas are also worth a try. There's a wide selection of beers, ideal people-watching opportunities on the pavement, and a lively bar scene upstairs.
☎ 210 361 6098
✉ Milioni 4 ☼ 10am-2am Ⓜ Syntagma

Kiku (7, E4) $$$$
Japanese
If you are going to eat Japanese in Athens, then Kiku offers some of the best – and some of the priciest – sushi in town. Ultra stylish and elegant, it has a sushi bar and exten-sive menu using fresh local fish and imported specialist ingredients. Bookings are advisable.
☎ 210 364 7033
✉ Dimokritou 12
☼ dinner Mon-Sat (closed Aug) Ⓜ Syn-tagma

Orizontes (6, B2) $$$$
Modern Mediterranean
You can't get any higher than this elegant upmarket restaurant on the hill with panoramic views over the Athens basin. One of the city's newer additions, the cuisine is Greek-influenced Mediterranean, with an emphasis on the sea. By all accounts the results are world class, with prices to match.
☎ 210 722 7065
✉ Lykavittos Hill
☼ lunch & dinner
🚕 taxi to funicular

Orizontes; world-class view, food and prices

Prytaneion (7, E5) $$$
Modern Italian
This chic restaurant-bar in one of Kolonaki's busy pedestrian thoroughfares has an inviting menu of pasta, seafood and steak dishes and a good selection of wine. There is a pleasant bar for a drink, or sit outside for the free fashion parade. Also on Plateia Kefalariou, Kifissia.
☎ 210 364 3353-4
✉ Milioni 7 ⏱ lunch & dinner Ⓜ Syntagma

To Ouzadiko (7, F5) $$
Mezedopolio
Tucked away in the Lemos Centre, To Ouzadiko offers refined traditional meze dishes and seasonal specials in a cosy setting. As the name suggests, there is also an extensive selection of ouzo. Bookings advisable.
☎ 210 729 5484
✉ Karneadou 25-29
⏱ lunch & dinner Tue-Sat Ⓜ Evangelismos

OMONIA

Athinaikon has spent 70 years perfecting its mezedhes

Athinaikon (7, C3) $
Mezedopolio
An institution in central Athens, offering a wide selection of traditional mezedhes and seafood dishes such as fried calamari or rice with mussels. The marble-top tables, old-style atmosphere (it's been around since 1932) and friendly service make this a popular place.
☎ 210 383 8485
✉ Themistokleous 2 (cnr Panepistimiou), Omonia
⏱ lunch & dinner

Mon-Sat (closed Aug)
Ⓜ Omonia

Bar Guru Bar (8, F1) $$$
Thai
For a spicy night out, this busy bar/restaurant near Athens market has an excellent Thai menu, funky décor, great music (late) and a hip crowd. There is live jazz some nights.
☎ 210 324 6530
✉ Plateia Theatrou 10, Omonia ⏱ dinner (closed Jul & Aug) Ⓜ Omonia

Diporto (7, B4) $
Mezedopolio
Go back in time at this quirky taverna near the Central Market. There is no signage, only two doors leading down to a rustic cellar where there's no menu, just a few dishes that haven't changed in years (try the chickpeas), washed down with the only wine – retsina (resinated white wine).
✉ Theatrou 1 (cnr Sofokleous), Omonia
⏱ 8am-7pm Mon-Sat
Ⓜ Omonia

Telis (8, F1) $
Taverna/Grillhouse
You can't get more basic than this fluoro-lit, bare-walled, paper-tablecloth Athens institution. Telis has been slaving over the flame grill cooking his famous pork chops to perfection since 1978. They come with chips and salad, washed down with house wine or beer. Don't even ask – there is nothing else on the menu.
☎ 210 324 2775
✉ Evripidou 86
⏱ breakfast, lunch & dinner (closed mid-Aug)
Ⓜ Monastiraki

Kid's Cuisine

Not many places in Athens have special children's meals or highchairs but most tavernas and restaurants are children-friendly, and it is common to see families out into the wee hours of the night.

Of course the trendier, more upmarket restaurants will not be impressed if you arrive with brat pack in tow, and the hours may be prohibitive in any case.

PLAKA & MONASTIRAKI

Byzantino (9, D3) $
Taverna
One of Plaka's better tavernas, it has traditional cuisine, excellent fish soup and plenty of *mageirefta*. You can sit outside in the busy square and watch the passing procession. It's good value and popular with tourists and locals year-round.
☎ 210 322 7368
✉ Kydathineon 18, Plaka ⏱ 9am-2am Mon-Sat Ⓜ Syntagma 🚻

Café Avyssinia (7, B5) $$
Music/Mezedopolio
In the heart of charmingly grungy Monastiraki Sq, the action at Café Avyssinia goes on long after the antique and junk dealers have gone home. It's a quirky place with live music and spontaneous floor shows. Best enjoyed on weekend afternoons for a late lunch.
☎ 210 321 7047
✉ Plateia Avyssinia, Monastiraki ⏱ closed Mon, Sat & Sun nights Ⓜ Monastiraki

Daphne's (9, D3) $$$
Mediterranean/International
One of the more sophisticated Plaka eateries in an impressive restored neoclassical mansion, Daphne's has frescoes on the walls reminiscent of Pompeii, and a pleasant courtyard for summer. The menu features regional specialities such as rabbit cooked in *mavrodaphne* wine and pork cooked with plums.
☎ 210 322 7971
✉ Lysikratous 4, Plaka

Dine alfresco or among the frescoes at Daphne's

⏱ dinner Ⓜ Syntagma; Akropoli

Orea Ellas (9, C1) $
Café/Ouzeri NO!
Escape the madness of Monastiraki by heading to the ouzeri on the 1st floor of the Centre for Hellenic Tradition (p62). There's a great selection of mezedhes to wash down with ouzo, or coffee and cake. Perfect for a light lunch during shopping or sightseeing expeditions.
☎ 210 321 3842
✉ Pandrosou 36 or Mitropoleos 59 (Arcade),

Monastiraki ⏱ 9am-6pm Ⓜ Monastiraki

O Damigos/Bakaliarika (9, D3) $
Taverna
This 1865 basement taverna, reputedly the oldest in Plaka, features in many old Greek movies. It's a lively winter place for traditional Greek fare, just mind your step. The house speciality is *bakaliaro*, salty cod fried in batter, served with lethal garlic dip. Try it.
☎ 210 322 5084
✉ Kydathineon 41,

Do You Want Smoke With That?

Greeks are amongst the biggest smokers in Europe, with nonsmokers seen as a bit of a curiosity. In October 2002, several strict anti-smoking measures were introduced but as is often the case, by the end of 2003 there was little evidence of compliance or enforcement, although a crackdown was expected during the Olympics.

All restaurants and most cafés should have at least half their tables designated as nonsmoking areas. Smoking is banned in taxis (good luck) and all indoor public areas.

Learn all there is to know about ouzo at Scholarheio

Plaka ☾ dinner (closed Jun-Aug) Ⓜ Akropoli; Syntagma

Palia Plakiotiki Taverna (9, D2) $
Taverna
The pleasant garden terrace of this old Plaka taverna (as the name translates) is always full in summer. The food is standard taverna but it's still one of the better places to eat in Plaka, with live music most nights.
☎ 210 322 8722 ✉ Lyssiou 26, Plaka ☾ dinner Ⓜ Akropoli; Monastiraki

✱ **Palia Taverna tou Psara (9, D2)** $
Seafood Taverna
A favourite haunt serving the best and cheapest

seafood in Plaka. This charming, renovated old taverna, in a 1898 house in the Anafiotika quarter, retains its great atmosphere and has a pleasant shaded courtyard for those hot summer days.
☎ 210 321 8733 ✉ Erehtheos 16 (cnr Erotokritou), Plaka ☾ 10am-1am Ⓜ Monastiraki

Platanos (9, D2) $
Taverna
This age-old taverna with tables in the courtyard under the giant plane tree is popular among Greeks and tourists. It serves delicious home-style fare, such as oven-baked potatoes, lamb fricassee and beef with quince and summer greens.

It gets very busy on a summer's night.
☎ 210 322 0666 ✉ Diogenous 4, Plaka ☾ lunch & dinner Mon-Sat Ⓜ Monastiraki

Scholarheio /Ouzeri Kouklis (9, D2) $
Ouzeri
There's atmosphere galore at this Plaka institution, once the area's first schoolhouse, now an old-style ouzeri with oak-beamed ceilings and marble tables. Choose from a simple but hearty range of mezedhes.
☎ 210 324 7605 ✉ Tripodon 14, Plaka ☾ lunch & dinner Mon-Fri Ⓜ Akropoli

To Kouti (8, F3) $$$
Modern Greek
Some outside tables have an Acropolis view but if you miss out, the food at this recently renovated, popular eatery is adequate consolation. The cute Greek menus are handwritten in children's books but plain English versions will help you select from a creative menu, with great salads and desserts.
☎ 210 321 3229 ✉ Adrianou 23, Thisio ☾ lunch & dinner Ⓜ Thisio

Dining to Impress

For a conventional business lunch environment in the centre, the **GB Corner** (☎ 210 333 0000) at the **Grand Bretagne** (p96) is a traditional meeting place for politicians and serious suits, with reasonable if pricey hotel fare, or the classy **Prytaneion** (p74) in Kolonaki. For a quintessentially Greek experience, try the classic, **Filippou** (p73).

If you want to really impress, you can't go wrong with the award-winning **Spondi** (p72).

PSIRI

Avalon (8, E2) $$
Bar/Restaurant
The atmosphere is part-Greek part-medieval, but the mussels are the main attraction, cooked with almost any spice and sauce you can imagine. The pleasant courtyard roof opens in summer, but this is a popular place year-round.
☎ 210 331 0572
✉ Leokoriou 20 (cnr Sarri) 🕒 dinner Tue-Sun, lunch Sun Ⓜ Monastiraki; Thisio

Il Cantuccio (8, E2) $$
Italian
Italians swear by this little slice of Italy in the midst of Psiri. Run by an Italian family who operate a pizzeria in Santorini in summer, the menu has excellent pasta and risotto dishes, including Sicilian specialities such as *pasta alla norma* and a delicious seafood pasta.
☎ 210 323 3670
✉ Lepeniotou (cnr Ivis) 🕒 dinner (closed summer) Ⓜ Monastiraki; Thisio

Kouzina-Cine Psiri (8, E2) $$$
Modern Greek/Mediterranean
Right next to the popular Cine Psiri outdoor cinema, this former factory has a warm atmosphere, friendly service and a creative menu. There's an impressive glass floor revealing the cellar, and a rooftop terrace with Acropolis views.
☎ 210 321 5534
✉ Sarri 40 🕒 dinner Ⓜ Thisio; Monastiraki

Wine and dine at To Krasopoulio tou Kokkora

To Krasopoulio tou Kokkora (8, F2) $$
Mezedopolio
Once a historic music taverna, the restaurant is decorated with collectables and old newspaper clippings. The tradition continues with live music every night and during Sunday lunch. The house speciality is chicken, grilled to perfection, and the salads are excellent.
☎ 210 321 1051
✉ Esopou 4 (cnr Karaiskaki) 🕒 dinner Ⓜ Monastiraki

To Zeidoron (8, F2) $$
Mezedopolio
One of the first trendy Psiri taverns, with outside tables for watching the passing promenade and a massive new extension on the back. There's a variety of mezedhes and interesting specials, although the standards can be inconsistent.
☎ 210 321 5368
✉ Agion Anargyron 17 (cnr Taki) 🕒 10am-2am Ⓜ Monastiraki

Taverna tou Psiri (8, F2) $
Taverna
One of Psiri's few remaining authentic tavernas, offering a range of tasty *mageirefta*. It's cheap and cheerful, with quirky murals and interesting old pictures on the walls to amuse you between courses.
☎ 210 321 4923 ✉ Aischilou 12 🕒 10am-2am Ⓜ Monastiraki

Vegetarian Delights

There are few dedicated vegetarian restaurants in Athens, but most tavernas will have plenty of salads and greens on the menu and Greek cuisine is big on vegetable dishes and legumes.

The **Eden Vegetarian Restaurant** (9, C2; ☎ 210 324 8858; Lyssiou 12, Plaka; 🕒 lunch & dinner Wed-Mon) in Plaka goes unchallenged as the best vegetarian restaurant in town. Soya products are substituted for meat in tasty vegetarian versions of moussaka (layers of baked eggplant) and other traditional favourites. It also has vegie burgers and organically produced beer and wine.

SYNTAGMA & THE CENTRE

Aigli (7, D6) $$$$
Mediterranean Café/ Restaurant
It's not just the setting in the Zappeio Gardens that makes this a great choice for summer or winter. Aigli has a fine menu of high standard, simple dishes presented with flair, as well as an extensive wine list. There are live outdoor jazz performances in summer.
☎ 210 336 9363-4
✉ Zappeio Gardens, Zappeio ⏱ lunch & dinner Ⓜ Syntagma

Aiolis (7, C5) $$$
Bar/Restaurant
Tucked in a pedestrian way, off the busy Ermou shopping strip, Aiolis is a great daytime pit stop. It has tables under the trees on the pavement, next to the Church of Agia Irini, and serves good pasta dishes, light meals and a good range of coffee, tea and milk shakes. It gets lively at night, occasionally with live music.
☎ 210 331 2839
✉ Eolou 23 (cnr Agia Irinis), Monastiraki ⏱ 10am-2am Ⓜ Monastiraki

Aigli prepares for the lunchtime rush

Body Fuel (7, D5) $
Deli/Café
A new addition to the fast-food scene, this is one of the few places you can get fresh salads, sushi, juices and gourmet sandwiches to takeaway – or there are tables upstairs. Great for a light lunch and there is a healthy breakfast spread of yogurt and cereal, too.
☎ 210 325 7772
✉ Stadiou 5, Syntagma ⏱ 10am-8pm Mon-Fri Ⓜ Syntagma

Cellier Le Bistrot (7, D5) $$
Greek/International
Run by leading wine merchants, Cellier, this is one of the few places with an extensive selection of Greek wines by the glass. It has an international feel and menu, with a choice of salads and lighter meals. Great for lunch.
☎ 210 363 8525
✉ Panepistimiou 10 (in Arcade), Syntagma ⏱ 10am-1am Ⓜ Syntagma

Furin Kazan (7, D5) $$
Japanese
Japanese tourists regularly fill this casual, café-style restaurant before a second shift of late-night Greek diners descend. The service can be a bit gruff, but the food makes up for it – quality (and relatively cheap) sushi and sashimi, as well as some delicious noodle dishes.
☎ 210 322 9170
✉ Apollonos 2, Syntagma ⏱ lunch & dinner Mon-Sat Ⓜ Syntagma

Noodle Bar (7, D5) $
Asian
Still a rarity in Athens, this small casual eatery has a range of tasty, if not inspiring, noodle dishes and Asian-style offerings at sensible prices. It also does a reasonable business in takeaway.
☎ 210 331 8585
✉ Apollonos 11, Syntagma ⏱ lunch & dinner Mon-Sat Ⓜ Syntagma

National Snack
Since the traditional Greek breakfast is often coffee and cigarettes, by mid-morning the stomach cries out for a snack – hence the *tiropita* (cheese pie), the standard fare offered by squillions of fast-food outlets and bakeries throughout Greece. For the best, fresh old-style *tiropites* in Athens (and many other tasty variations) head to **Ariston** (7, D5; ☎ 210 322 7626; Voulis 10, Syntagma).

SEAFOOD

Dourambeis (5, E2) $$$
Taverna
An enduring seafront taverna in Piraeus, you can get fresh fish here grilled to perfection and served with a simple oil and lemon dressing, as well as wonderful crayfish soup.
☎ 210 412 2092 ✉ Akti Dilaveri 27, Piraeus ☽ lunch & dinner 🚖 taxi

Jimmy & the Fish (5, E3) $$$
Restaurant
It's hard to go past the lobster spaghetti and other seafood pastas that are house specialities, along with an excellent daily catch of fresh fish. One of the more stylish places among the fish tavernas that line Mikrolimano, Jimmy's has a great range of entrées, including stuffed calamari, and ouzo and sesame prawns.
☎ 210 412 4417 ✉ Akti Koumoundourou 46, Mikrolimano, Piraeus ☽ lunch & dinner 🚖 taxi

Lambros (1, B3) $$$
Taverna
Founded in 1889 during the reign of King George I, Lambros was cooking fish when seaside Vouliagmeni was a day trip from Athens. The expanded, upmarket restaurant of today, right on the water, is still a favourite Sunday lunch spot for Athenians.
☎ 210 896 0144 ✉ Poseidonos 20 (opposite Limni Vouliagmenis),

Vouliagmeni ☽ lunch & dinner 🚖 taxi

✳ Ta 5 Piata (5, A1) $
Ouzeri
With an established serious fish tavern across the road, Tassos Kollias opened this casual eatery in 2003 to offer a different dining experience. Delicious rounds of five plates of seafood mezedhes (thus the name) are served at €10 a pop. Stop ordering when you have had enough. It's tricky to get to so make sure the taxi driver has a street directory.
☎ 210 461 8808 ✉ Plastira 3 & 8, Piraeus (near cnr Kalokairinou & Dramas) ☽ lunch & dinner (closed Sun night) 🚖 taxi

Trata o Stelios (7, F6) $$$
Taverna
Once the communist stronghold of Athens, the neighbourhood of Kaisariani has become more associated with the excellent

seafood tavernas on the main square. Stelios is the most popular seafood ouzeri in the square, with a daily catch of fresh fish and tasty mezedhes. It's a short taxi ride from town (stop here after visiting the nearby monastery; see p28).
☎ 210 729 1533 ✉ Plateia Anagenniseos 7-9, Kaisariani ☽ lunch & dinner 🚖 taxi

Varoulko (5, E1) $$$$
Mediterranean
An exquisite dining experience at the hands of Lefteris Lefterou, the country's only home-grown Michelin chef. The squid ink soup is among the refined seafood creations at this renowned Piraeus restaurant. In summer, Varoulko moves to the waterfront (☎ 210 411 2043, Vouliagmenis Marina).
☎ 210 422 1283 ✉ Deligeorgi 14, Piraeus ☽ dinner Mon-Sat (closed Jul-Aug) 🚖 taxi

Eating Late

For a memorable Athens experience after a big night out, go into the darkened central meat market, where the tavernas turn out huge pots and trays of tasty, traditional home-style dishes, 24 hours a day.

An eclectic clientele includes truckies, hungry market workers and elegant couples emerging from local clubs and bars at 5am in search of a bowl of hangover-busting steaming *patsa* (tripe soup) or pig-trotter soup. Exiting at dawn as market traders start hanging meat out is truly surreal. Try **Taverna Papandreou** (8, F1; ☎ 210 321 4970; Aristogeitonos 1, Monastiraki).

WORTH THE TRIP

Biftekoupoli-George's Steakhouse (4, B1) $
Grillhouse
Since George's opened in 1951, a row of grillhouses serving *biftekia* (tasty Greek burger-come-meatballs) opened here, earning the area the moniker *biftek-oupoli* (burgerland). Great value grilled meats, salads and appetisers.
☎ 210 8942041 ✉ **Konstantinoupoleos 4-6, Glyfada** ☽ **lunch & dinner** 🚗 **A2 or** 🚕 **taxi**

Gefsis me Onomasies Proelefsis (3, B1) $$$
Modern Greek
A stylish restaurant in a renovated mansion, specialising in traditional dishes based on regional ingredients, prepared with a sophisticated, modern touch.
☎ 210 800 1402 ✉ **Kifissias 317, Kifissia** ☽ **dinner Mon-Sat** 🚕 **taxi**

Tour Greece in just a couple of hours at Ta Kioupia

Plous Podilatou (5, E2) $$$
Seafood/Mediterranean
Year-round sister restaurant of the pioneering *nuevo*-Greek Kitrino Podilato offers elegant dining on the picturesque Mikrolimano harbour, with an emphasis on seafood.
☎ 210 413 7910 ✉ **Akti Koumoundourou 42, Piraeus** ☽ **dinner** 🚕 **taxi**

Ta Kioupia (1, C1) $$$$
Modern/Traditional Greek
Ta Kioupia is a smorgasbord of Greek cuisine, from the islands to the regions, from modern to classic dishes. The setting is impressive and there is a cheaper set menu, as well as à la carte dining.
☎ 210 620 0005 ✉ **Plateia Politias, Kifissia** ☽ **dinner Mon-Sat, lunch Sun** 🚕 **taxi**

Tselementes (5, F1) $$
Greek/International
Run by relatives of Nikos Tselementes, who wrote Greece's controversial but famous cookbook, this fine restaurant has a homy atmosphere and serves food from the book.
☎ 210 940 5135 ✉ **Aeroporon 10, Palio Faliro** ☽ **lunch & dinner** 🚗 **A1** 🚕 **taxi**

Vardis (3, C1) $$$$
Modern French/Mediterranean
Greece's first Michelin star restaurant, Vardis is the big splurge in Athens' gastronomic scene. Located in the Pentelikon hotel (p97), its food and service are simply exquisite.
☎ 210 628 1660 ✉ **Deligianni 66, Kefalari** ☽ **dinner Mon-Sat** 🚕 **taxi**

Dining Like the Ancients

Athens is not big on theme restaurants but it was only a matter of time before someone turned to ancient Greece for inspiration – and gimmicks. **Archaion Gefsis** (7, A3; ☎ 210 523 9661; Kodratou 22, Metaxourgio, or 5,E3; ☎ 210 413 8617; Epidavrou 10, Mikrolimano Piraeus; ☽ lunch & dinner Mon-Sat) gives new meaning to the term retro.

Roast meats and fish prevail, served with purées of peas or chickpeas and vegetables. The ancient theme even extends to both the décor and service. Diners are seated at solid wooden tables, served by waiters in flowing red robes. There are no glasses (the ancients used earthenware cups), and spoons instead of forks. Bookings essential.

CAFÉS & SWEET TREATS

Despite the inexplicably obscene price of coffee (up to €4.60, although the average is €3.50), the Athens café society is still going strong; drinking coffee seems to be the national pastime. Old-style coffee houses serving the heavy Greek brew are becoming rare these days, but there is no shortage of trendy cafés. DeCapo in the café-mecca square on Kolonaki has a reputation for the best coffee in town, but if you can't get a seat, there are plenty of options around the square and on nearby Milioni, not to mention the rest of town. Sweet tooths will be more than satisfied with local delights.

Aigaion – Homer Simpson's favourite Athens café

Aigaion (6, B3) $
Sweets
Since 1826, this basement haunt has offered one of the cheapest sweet treats in Athens. Huge fryers dish out an endless supply of *loukoumades* (Greek-style doughnuts) served with honey and walnuts. There are also other pastries, including cheese pies and rice pudding.
☎ 210 381 4621
✉ Panepistimiou 46, Athens ⊙ 8am-11pm (closed Sun) Ⓜ Omonia

Klepsidra (9, C2)   GREAT! $
Café/Sweets
A cosy café overlooking Anafiotika, with homemade Greek sweets (try the walnut pie with ice cream) and speciality dairy products. The *spanakopita* (spinach pie) is served with fresh yogurt and there are treats such as iced mountain tea.
☎ 210 321 8726
✉ Thrasyvoulou 9 (cnr Klepsidra), Plaka ⊙ summer 9am-1am, winter 10am-midnight Ⓜ Monastiraki ♿

Melina (9, D2) $
Café
A quaint café dedicated to Greece's legendary actress and politician, the late Melina Mercouri. There's interesting memorabilia and photographs, china tea

sets and a cosy yet formal, old-world style.
☎ 210 324 6501 ✉ Lyssiou 22, Plaka ⊙ noon-late Ⓜ Monastiraki

Varsos (3, B2) $
Patisserie/Café
A Kifissia landmark, this huge patisserie has been making high-quality traditional Greek sweets and dairy products since 1892. Walk past the trays of goodies to the old-style café or sit in the outside courtyard and try the famous rice pudding, honeyed pastries, yogurt or scrumptious cheese pies – and the best value coffee in Kifissia.
☎ 210 801 3743 ✉ Kassaveti 5, Kifissia ⊙ 7am-1am Ⓜ Kifissia ♿

Tristrato (9, E3) $
Café
This little gem off Plaka's busy square specialises in milk-based desserts and has a wonderful traditional feel. There's a great selection of herbal and mountain teas, milk shakes and wicked hot chocolate with cognac. Prices are a little steep.
☎ 210 324 4472
✉ Angelou Geronta (cnr Dedalou), Plaka ⊙ 10am-1am Ⓜ Syntagma ♿

Fancy a Frappé?

Nescafé pulled off the biggest coup in Greece with the invention of the frappé (a frothy version of iced coffee made with this instant brew) that you see everyone sipping for hours on end. For real coffee, try the *freddo* espresso versions.

If there's one thing Greeks pride themselves on, it's their ability to have a good time. Some years back, the government tried to impose stricter closing times on nightclubs to boost the country's productivity, but a virtual rebellion put a stop to that and Athenians happily party to all hours.

What to Wear?

Athenians like to dress up for a night out and the more stylish the place, the more you are likely to feel uncomfortable if you rock up looking like a backpacker. In the really upmarket bars and clubs, which have strict 'face control', you may get turned away at the door, especially if you are in a big group of men or don't have a fancy car. Dress to impress.

Tavernas, bars and restaurants in tourist areas are more relaxed but smart casual wear is recommended.

There's a tremendous range of bars (and *barakia*, the cosier variety), music venues and clubs, from rock to jazz, Greek pop and folk music. Greek music thrives in all its contemporary and traditional forms, but Athens also hosts rock and blues festivals and some impressive international touring acts.

The cultural calendar's highlight is the Athens Festival, which features leading international performers, orchestras, theatre and dance troupes.

There is also a thriving theatre tradition – ancient, mainstream and experimental – but as performances are mostly in Greek, we have not emphasised theatre here. For clubbers, Athens offers a vibrant dance club scene, with more stamina than most other cities and top international DJs.

As with restaurants, the entertainment scene starts late; most clubs are empty before midnight, and only start filling after 1am. Going out isn't cheap, and even if there's no door charge, rest assured the drinks bill will make up for it (although the serves are usually doubles).

Top Acts Top the Billing

You really have to be in Athens between October and April to see the country's best contemporary artists perform. In summer, most big acts go on international tours and work the festival circuit around Greece. Most perform in modern cabaret-style venues, where you can sit at tables or the bar, rather than in a stiff concert setting. They are fairly pricey and start very late. Ask around for the best shows in town.

Key venues include converted theatre **Rex** (7, C3; ☎ 210 381 4591; Panepistimiou 48), modern **Iera Odos** (8, C2; ☎ 210 342 8272; Iera Odos 18, Gazi; €20) and **Zygos** (9, D3; ☎ 210 324 1610; Kydathineon 22, Plaka; €15 incl 1st drink) where you can watch the show from the top-floor bar. **Diogenis Studio** (7, B8; ☎ 210 943 5754; Syngrou 259) is set up like a theatre. The big pop acts are Anna Vissi, Despina Vandi, Notis Sfakianakis, Ploutarhos and the popular George Dalaras. More *entekna* artists include Pyx Lax, Yiannis Kotsiras, Eleftheria Arvanitaki, Alkistis Protopsalti and Savina Yannatou.

Special Events

6 January *Epiphany* – the blessing of the water takes place in Piraeus, where young men dive in to retrieve a cross thrown into the sea. The winner is blessed with good luck for the year

February *Apokries* – the Greek Carnivale, when fancy-dress parties are held all over town and revellers run riot in Plaka

February/March *Ash Monday* – at the beginning of Lent, Athenians fly kites on Filopappos Hill, Lykavittos Hill and parks around the city

25 March *Greek National Day* – full military parade in the city along Akadimias every second year (schools parade on alternate years)

March/April *Easter* – night church services including a candlelit procession on Good Friday and midnight services on Easter Saturday

May *Spring* – the arrival of spring is celebrated by going to mountains and collecting wildflowers to make wreaths, which are hung in doorways

June–September *Athens Festival* – music, dance and drama in venues around Athens, the main venue being the Theatre of Herodes Atticus (see p84)
Epidauros Festival – ancient Greek drama festival at the ancient Theatre of Epidauros (see p84)

July *Rockwave* – Greece's biggest annual rock music festival, with three days of nonstop music by some top international acts. Tickets from TicketHellas (☎ 210 618 9300; www.didimusic.gr)

28 October *Ohi Day* – military parade, celebrating the rejection of the Italian ultimatum in 1940

CLASSICAL MUSIC, OPERA & DANCE

Dora Stratou Dance Theatre (7, A7)
Traditional folk dancing shows on Filopappos Hill are a summer tradition. More than 75 musicians and dancers present dances from around Greece in a colourful 90-minute show. Some of the elaborate costumes are museum pieces. If you get really inspired, inquire about their dance workshops.
☎ 210 324 4395, theatre 210 921 4650
⌨ www.grdance.org
✉ Filopappos Hill
€ €13 ⏱ 9.30pm Tue-Sat, 8.15pm Sun May-Sep
Ⓜ Akropoli

Megaron – Athens Concert Hall (6, D2)
The impressive Megaron is one of Europe's most state-of-the-art concert halls, with superb acoustics and excellent facilities, recently expanded to include an exhibition hall and library. It presents a rich winter programme of operas and concerts featuring world-class international and Greek artists and performers.

Megaron has world-class acoustics and performers

☎ 210 728 2333-7
⌨ www.megaron.gr
✉ Vasilissis Sofias, Ambelokipi (programme & tickets also at Omirou 8, 10am-4pm Mon-Fri)
Ⓜ Megaro Moussikis
€ varies; discounts for students & under 18s; book in advance ✖ Allegro (☎ 210 728 2150)

National Theatre of Greece (7, B3)
This is the country's pre-eminent company, acclaimed for classic ancient Greek tragedies. In summer, performances are held throughout Greece and during the Athens and Epidauros Festivals (see below). In winter, the historic theatre plays host to the leading theatre troupes in Greece. Only one annexe of the theatre was open during recent major earthquake repair work.
☎ 210 522 3242
⌨ www.n-t.gr ✉ Agiou Konstantinou 22, Omonia
€ varies Ⓜ Omonia

Olympia Theatre/Opera House (6, A2)
The Greek National Opera (Ethniki Lyriki Skini) season runs from November to June. Performances of ballet and opera are held at the Olympia Theatre or Herodes Atticus in summer.
☎ 210 360 0180, box office 210 361 2461
⌨ www.national opera.gr ✉ Akadimias 59, Athens € varies
Ⓜ Panepistimio

Festive Athens
Every summer, performances from leading international and Greek acts, from the New York Ballet to Andrea Bocelli, take place under the stars at the ancient Theatre of Herodes Atticus, the main venue of the Athens Festival. Events are held from June to September. For programme information and tickets, contact the **Hellenic Festival box office** (☎ 210 322 1459; www.hellenicfestival.gr; Panepistimiou 39).

The festival also runs the **Epidauros Festival** in July and August, which presents ancient Greek tragedy, comedy and satire at the ancient Theatre of Epidauros, two hours from Athens. Set in lush surrounds, the theatre has incredible acoustics, so much so that you can hear a pin drop on the stage from the top rows. There are buses direct to the theatre or you can take a dinner and cruise option for a special treat.

LIVE MUSIC

Alavastron Café (7, F8)
It can feel like there's a band in your lounge room in this cosy and casual world-music bar, which hosts regular appearances by eclectic musicians, including the inspirational Armenian Haig Hazdjian. There are snacks, a lounge area and a great atmosphere.
☎ 210 756 0102
✉ Damareos 78, Pangrati
€ €12-16 (incl 1st drink) for a band ⌚ 10pm-late Tue-Sat 🚇 4

Gargarin 205 Live Music Space (7, B1)
One of the newer live rock music venues where some of the top international touring acts play, as well as local groups of various musical persuasions.
☎ 210 8547601
✉ Liossion 205, Thi-marakia 24 € varies
⌚ from 9.30pm
Ⓜ Attiki

Half Note Jazz Club (7, D8)
A stylish venue with an international line-up playing classic jazz, folk and occasional Celtic music. It's the original and best venue in Athens for serious jazz. Book a table or you can stand at the bar.
☎ 210 921 3310
🖥 www.half.note.gr
✉ Trivonianou 17, Mets
€ €25-30 ⌚ 10.30pm
🚇 2, 11

House of Art (8, E2)
A well-established live music theatre, with changing themes and artists from Greek *laika* and *entekna* to Latin, blues, jazz and even poetry and theatrical performances.
☎ 210 321 7678
✉ Sahtouri 4 (cnr Sarri), Psiri € €18
⌚ performances start 10.30pm
Ⓜ Monastiraki

Palenque (6, F1)
A slice of Havana in Athens, there's regular live music, with artists from around the world, salsa parties and flamenco shows. You can take tango lessons earlier in the evenings – and taste the best margaritas in town.
☎ 210 775 2360
🖥 www.palenque.gr
✉ Farandaton 41, Ambelokipi € €10
⌚ 9.30-late
Ⓜ Ambelokipi 🚇 8, 13

Rodon Club (7, C2)
Top-name rock bands, as well as soul and reggae acts, perform in this classic venue in a converted movie theatre most Fridays and Saturdays. It's just north of Omonia Sq. Check listings for what's playing.
☎ 210 524 7427
✉ Marni 24, Omonia
€ varies
⌚ from 10pm (for performances) 🚇 5

Put on your dancing shoes and head out for a night at Palenque

GREEK MUSIC

The bouzouki may be the first thing that comes to mind when you think of Greek music but these days you can hear Greek clubbing music, pop, heavy metal, rap and even country and western.

Live performances of traditional *laika* (popular music) are still widespread, as is *rebetika* (the Greek equivalent of the blues) and modern *entekna* (meaning 'artistic' or quality music). Pop and dance hits with a disco-*tsifteteli* beat are also popular – and the *bouzoukia* are still going strong. Warning: there may be no door charge at many live music places, but the drinks are expensive and there may be a minimum consumption charge.

Boemissa (7, D2)
A *rebetika* staple that plays more *laika* these days, Boemissa is usually lively and raucous, with the dancing moving onto the tables late into the night.
☎ 210 384 3836
✉ Solomou 19, Exarhia
🕐 11pm-late (closed Aug) 🚕 taxi

Mnisikleous (9, C2)
A classic Plaka taverna, popular for its live music (Thursday to Sunday), it has a full-sized stage and dance floor and gets very lively. A good place for traditional music and dancing if you can't face a nightclub or *rebetadiko*.

Greek-style grunge at Rebetiki Istoria

Smashing Plates

Despite the popular perception, there is not much plate-smashing to be had in Greece these days. It's not the done thing in restaurants and in the big cabaret-style *bouzoukia* clubs the way to revel and blow your euros is to buy trays of carnations and shower your dancing friends or the singers.

At some bars, party animals throw stacks of paper napkins everywhere when the night heats up. Be warned, these acts of merrymaking can be very pricey (you pay for the napkins!).

☎ 210 322 5558
✉ Mnisikleous 22 (cnr Lyssiou), Plaka 🕐 9pm-late (10.30pm-late Fri & Sat) Ⓜ Monastiraki

Mousikes Skies (7, F7)
An intimate venue run by a charming singer-bouzouki player couple with a programme of *laika*, *entekna* and *rebetika* music and an arty crowd. There's a range of mezedhes and an outdoor courtyard in summer.
☎ 210 756 1465
✉ Athanasias 4, Pangrati 🕐 8pm-late (closed Aug) 🚌 2, 4, 11

Rebetiki Istoria (7, F2)
One of the older *rebetika* haunts, with an authentic grungy, smoky atmosphere, dedicated regulars and a wall of old photos of *rebetika* musicians. It's casual, relaxed, affordable and thus popular with students.
☎ 210 642 4937
✉ Ippokratous 181, Exarhia 🕐 11pm-late

Stoa Athanaton (7, C4)
In the middle of Athens Market, this classic *rebetadiko* has been around since 1930. It is open day and night and is always lively, with veteran *rebetes* and loyal patrons. There's decent food, too.
☎ 210 321 4362
✉ Sofokleous 19 & Stoa Athanaton (arcade), Central Market, Omonia
🕐 3-7.30pm & 11pm-late Mon-Sat Ⓜ Omonia

Taximi (7, E3) Most of Greece's major *rebetika* exponents have played here since it opened 20 years ago at the beginning of the *rebetika* revival. It's gone a little upmarket – and expensive – but it is still a popular and authentic venue that is packed most weekends.
☎ 210 363 9919
✉ cnr Trikoupi Harilaou & Isavron 29, Neapoli
◷ 11pm-late Thu-Sun
🚕 taxi

In the Doghouse

The *bouzoukia*, commonly called *skyladika* (dog-houses) because of the crooning singers, are a Greek institution, but not everyone's cup of tea. Pricey, smoky and a tad sleazy, with B-grade performers, they are nonetheless packed out most nights.

If you are game, try veteran **Romeo** (7, D7; ☎ 210 922 4885; Kallirrois 4; summer: ☎ 210 894 5345; Ellinikou 1, Glyfada). Be warned, it can be outrageously expensive, especially if you sit at a table, with bottles of whisky sold at exorbitant prices. Not for the faint-hearted.

BARS

Athens has a disproportionate number of bars, from mellow watering holes to pumping night spots – and everything in between (and often all-in-one). Many also serve coffee and food. In winter the liveliest bars are in Kolonaki, Psiri, Gazi and the inner city. In summer, the action migrates to Piraeus and the coast, with bars along the waterfront from Palio Faliro to Varkiza, although many city bars have terraces or outdoor courtyards. Late night bars often have a €7-plus door charge, which includes your first drink.

Baila (6, C3) A popular spot in the trendy bar strip on the pedestrianised section of Haritos, which has patrons spilling out on to the road most nights. This is one the liveliest nightspots in Kolonaki.
☎ 210 723 3019
✉ Haritos 43, Kolonaki
◷ 9pm-late
Ⓜ Evangelismos

Baroc'e (7, E6) Right next to the old Olympic Stadium, this cool 'club restaurant' spills out onto the pavement in summer. It's open all day but comes into its own at night, with a resident DJ and regular procession of well-heeled Athenians.
☎ 210 752 1768

✉ Agras & Vasileos Konstantinou, Mets (next to Stadium) ◷ 10am-late Ⓜ Syntagma
🚌 2, 4, 11

Bee (8, F3) Popular with the arty, alternative set, this bar restaurant has excellent food, interesting and constantly changing

décor and displays. It is a gay-friendly hang-out where the hip young crowd spills out on to the street most nights.
☎ 210 321 2624
✉ Miaouli & Themidos, Psiri ◷ 8pm-1am, lunch from noon Sat & Sun (closed Mon)
Ⓜ Monastiraki

The dancefloor awaits you at Bee

Brettos has plenty
of soul and spirits

Brettos (9, D3) A Plaka
landmark, this quaint little
bar has a stunning backlit
wall of coloured bottles, old
wine barrels along another
wall and a refreshingly old-
fashioned feel. It's a spirits
shop by day and a quiet
spot for a nightcap, with a
tempting range of home-
made brews.
☎ 210 323 2110
✉ Kydathineon 41,
Plaka ⏱ 10am-midnight
Ⓜ Syntagma

Briki (6, E2) This tiny bar
often gets so busy the crowd
spills out on to Plateia
Mavili – one of Athens'
biggest night-time drinking

holes, where revellers from
adjoining bars meet around
the fountain. It's one of the
most popular low-key and
friendly bars in town.
☎ 210 645 2380
✉ Doryleou 6, Plateia
Mavili, Ambelokipi
⏱ midnight-3.30am
Ⓜ Ambelokipi

Café Folie (6, F1) A cosy,
established and popular bar
with colourful, funky décor,
Folie attracts a mixed and
friendly crowd, with music
ranging from reggae to
ethnic. Things get lively late
but if you need more space,
head next door to Folie's
full-on dance club.
☎ 210 646 9852
✉ Eslin 4, Ambelokipi
⏱ 10.30am-late; club
11pm-late Mon-Sat
Ⓜ Ambelokipi

De Luxe (7, C7) Funky '60s-
airport décor, an innovative
menu and an alternative
hip young crowd make this
a fun place for a drink or a
meal. A great mix of music
and friendly bar team.
☎ 210 924 3184
✉ Falirou 15, Makri-
gianni ⏱ 9pm-late
(dinner to 1.30am)
Ⓜ Akropoli

Fidelio (8, E2) A creative
space with lots of stone and
wood, the front courtyard
bar opens completely in
summer, with bar stools
on the pavement and the
casual crowd spilling onto
the street.
☎ 210 321 2977
✉ Ogygou 2 (cnr
Navarhou Apostoli), Psiri
⏱ 9.30pm-3.30am
Ⓜ Thisio

Inoteka (8, E3) You might
wonder what you are doing
as you head down the dark
alley towards the deserted
Monastiraki Flea Market,
but persevere and amid the
closed antique stalls you
will find a casual, candlelit
bar playing great free-style
music.
☎ 210 324 6446
✉ Plateia Avyssinias 3,
Monastiraki ⏱ 1pm-late
Ⓜ Monastiraki

Micraasia Lounge (8, B2)
In summer there's a great
lounge on the terrace, but
this trendy bar with an
east-meets-west fusion
in both décor and music
is a good option year-
round. The place to come
for ethnic music, from
Turk-Arab beats to Latin,
with well-regarded theme
nights.
☎ 210 346 4851
✉ Konstandinoupoleos
70, Gazi ⏱ 10pm-
3.30am 🚕 taxi

Mike's Irish Bar (6, F1)
Mike's not Irish but you
can still hear live Irish
music, as well as classic
rock and blues most nights.
There's Guinness on tap

and a mixed crowd.
☎ 210 777 6797 ✉ Sinopis 6, Athens Tower, Ambelokipi € free (charge for live bands) 🕑 8pm-late 🚌 13

Rock'n'Roll (6, C3) It's a bit loud for a restaurant (the food is decent) but the veteran bar rocks most and is popular with the arts set and older crowd. Face control can be strict.
☎ 210 721 7127 ✉ Loukianou 6 (cnr Ypsilandou, Kolonaki) 🕑 9pm-late (closed summer) Ⓜ Evangelismos

Skoufaki (6, A2) This cosy bar is great for a coffee and snack or a quiet drink during the day. In the evening it livens up with a more upbeat trendy crowd and cool music. If it's full, a string of new funky bars has opened further up Skoufa, away from the square.
☎ 210 364 5888 ✉ Skoufa 47-49, Kolonaki 🕑 11am-3am (later Fri & Sat) Ⓜ Syntagma

Soul (8, F1) This bar-restaurant in a restored neoclassical building has a lively bar, a small club on the second level, a fine restaurant with an innovative menu and a lush green courtyard in summer. There's an arty crowd, good cocktails and a friendly atmosphere.
☎ 210 331 0907 ✉ Evripidou 65, Psiri 🕑 9.30pm-3.30am Ⓜ Monastiraki

Stavlos, another of Athens' historic sights

Stavlos (8, D3) Located in the old royal stables, this is one of the originals in the happening Thisio bar and café strip. There's a great internal courtyard bar and tables on the pavement outside. It is also a popular alternative rock venue that attracts all ages.
☎ 210 346 7206 ✉ Iraklidon 10, Thisio 🕑 10am-4am Ⓜ Thisio

Thirio (8, E2) A two-level warren of small rooms, lounges and bars, the Lilliputian Thirio (Greek for giant) is funky and fun, and the music ranges from acid jazz to ethnic. It can get very crowded.
☎ 210 722 4104 ✉ Lepeniotou 1, Psiri 🕑 8pm-late Ⓜ Monastiraki

Wunderbar (7, D2) A trendy lounge bar and café right on busy Plateia Exarhia, this is a good place to start if you want to discover this cool, student-bohemian neighbourhood of Athens. There are plenty of casual, cool and cheap (relatively) bars and eateries nearby.
☎ 210 381 8577 ✉ Themistokleous 80, Exarhia 🕑 10am-late Ⓜ Omonia

Beer, Beer & More Beer

There aren't many English-style pubs in Greece but **Craft Athens** (6, E1; ☎ 210 646 2350; Alexandras 205, Ambelokipi; 🕑 10am-1.30am Sun-Fri, 10am-2am Sat) is a full-on microbrewery where you can sit among the industrial machinery that brews six different beers, including an ale called 'Swedish Blonde'. There's an eclectic restaurant and regular tours and tastings.

SUMMER NIGHTSPOTS

Acai (7, D7) With a great rooftop terrace with views of the Acropolis and Lykavittos Hill, this popular spot (formerly Exo) attracts a hip mixed-age crowd. It is one of the staple drinking holes of an Athenian summer.
☎ 210 923 5818
✉ **Markou Mousourou 1, Mets** € €10 (Fri & Sat €15) 🕙 9pm-late
🚌 2, 4, 11

Akrotiri Lounge (1, B3) This lounge bar 'club restaurant' is in an impressive setting right on the beach. It can fit 3500 people and is renowned for huge dance parties on weekends with top international and resident DJs.
☎ 210 985 9147 ✉ **Vas Georgiou B 5, Agios Kosmas** € €10 🕙 9pm-late 🚇 A2

Bedlam (7, E6) A stylish and cool (literally) bar in the middle of the Zappeio Gardens, set among the trees, with lounges, and everchanging décor – in 2003 it was African theme. There's multi-ethnic food, mainstream music and a slick crowd.
☎ 210 336 9340-1
✉ **Zappeio Gardens, Syntagma** € €10 (Fri & Sat €15) 🕙 9pm-late
Ⓜ Syntagma

Island (1, B3) A stunning seaside club, with Cycladic island décor and an ultra-glam crowd. It's a long way to go to be turned away by

Things warm up as the day cools down at Istioploikos

the 'face control' – booking for a romantic dinner is your best bet, then stay for a drink as the place hots up.
☎ 210 965 3563-4
✉ **Limanakia Vouliagmenis, Varkiza** € €13
🕙 midnight-late 🚕 taxi

Istioploikos (5, E3) This popular bar-restaurant, part of the Piraeus Yacht Club, is on a moored restored ship at the western end of Mikrolimano Harbour, with great panoramic views. The top deck bar (a café by day) gets lively until late.
☎ 210 413 4084 ✉ **Akti Mikrolimanou, Piraeus** € €8 (Fri & Sat €10) 🕙 10am-3.30am 🚕 taxi

Liberty Come Back (1, B3) One of the closer beach side clubs, with lounge music and R&B early on and more mainstream, pop and some Greek later into the night. It's popular with the younger set.
☎ 210 982 1200 ✉ **Poseidonos 22, Floisvos Park, Palio Faliro** € €7 (Fri & Sat €10) 🕙 9pm-late
Ⓜ Faliro 🚇 A1

On the Road (7, D7) This long and narrow bar restaurant 'on the road' is

a patch of green between two busy thoroughfares. It turns into a happening bar at night, with cosy corners, food and full-on dance areas with guest DJs and the latest club music.
☎ 210 347 8716
✉ **Ardittou 1, Mets**
€ €7 (Fri & Sat €10)
🕙 9pm-late 🚌 2, 4, 11

Skipper's (1, B3) The tall mast at the rear of Kalamaki marina will lead you to this casual all-day bar, decked out like a ship (a five-minute walk from the main road). Popular with locals and visiting yachts, it's great for an evening drink and gets livelier late.
☎ 210 988 0282
✉ **Pier 1, Kalamaki Marina, Kalamaki** 🕙 open all day 🚇 A2 🚕 taxi

Theatro Floisvos (1, B3) This beachfront restaurant-bar, in the former summer palace of King Otto and Amalia, is superbly located along the Faliro esplanade. Ideal for sunset drinks, it attracts a mixed crowd.
☎ 210 981 4245
✉ **Poseidonos (opposite 33), Palio Faliro** 🕙 café all day, bar 9pm-3am
🚇 A1

DANCE CLUBS

Envy (1, C2) One of a number of spin-offs from the original Envy, this club attracts the glam crowd northern suburbs set (the 'face control' is strict) and plays pop and mainstream music. In summer, Envy moves to the beach, although the venue constantly changes.
☎ 210 689 8560
✉ Kifissias 7, Maroussi
€ €10 (Fri & Sat € 15)
🕙 11pm-3.30am

Free2Go (7, D7) One of the liveliest mainstream clubs, in a multi-function venue renowned for themed music nights. It's right next door to Prime, which has more of a Greek music leaning these days (although the trends change as often as the venues).
☎ 210 924 9814
✉ Vouliagmenis 22, Neos Kosmos € Fri/Sat €7.50/11.50 🕙 11pm-late 🚖 taxi

Kalua (7, D5) A classic mainstream downtown club with the latest dance music (and occasional Greek club music), where there is usually pandemonium until dawn and an under-30s crowd.
☎ 210 360 8304
✉ Amerikis 6, Syntagma € €12 (Sat €15)
🕙 11pm-late
Ⓜ Syntagma

Memphis (6, D3) An established tourist-friendly Athenian bar in a strip behind the Hilton, Memphis plays mainstream '80s and '90s classics, as well as the latest chart successes. The crowd is generally mixed age.
☎ 210 722 4104
✉ Ventiri 5 🕙 Tue-Sun Ⓜ Evangelismos

Plus Soda (8, D2) A multi-level club with huge dance floor, and a regular line-up of top guest DJs. One for young, hardcore clubbers, the music is progressive/psychedelic trance, house and techno – and the lights and pace are not for the faint-hearted.
☎ 210 345 6187
✉ Ermou 161, Thisio
€ €11.50 (more for guest DJs) 🕙 from midnight til late Wed-Sun Ⓜ Thisio

U-Matic (7, D9) On Saturday night this club competes with the best in Europe, with top resident and international guest DJs. Super-industrial design inside and out, it is a little out of the way but popular with hardcore clubbers.

☎ 6945363700
✉ Vouliagmenis 268, Neos Kosmos € €12
🕙 11pm-late Fri-Sun
🚖 taxi

Venue (8, F2) Resident DJs keep this longstanding place buzzing with house, progressive and techno dance tunes. The party atmosphere follows to Venue's massive summer dance venue (30km Athens–Sounion Rd, Varkiza; ☎ 210 897 0333).
☎ 210 331 7801
✉ Agias Eleousis & Kakourgiodikeio, Monastiraki
€ €10 🕙 9pm-late Wed-Sat Ⓜ Monastiraki

Vinilio (1, B3) The only dedicated 'disco' in town, this place is packed with tourists and locals of all ages wanting an old-fashioned boogie to '60s, '70s and '80s music. In the Emmantina Hotel along the coast.
☎ 210 968 1056
✉ Poseidonos 33, Glyfada € €8 (Fri & Sat €12)
🕙 Tue-Sun 🚌 A2

Alternatives

Alternative music fans can find their brand of dark or electro-clash, alternative rock, indie rock, electronica, even gothic and underground music at a number of venues around town. Here's a few of the leading lights of the alternative scene.

Decadence (7, E2; ☎ 210 882 3544; ✉ Voulgaroktonou 69, cnr Pouliherias, Lofos Strefi)
Mad (8, B2; ☎ 210 345 4604; ✉ Persefonis & Dekeleon 12, Gazi)
Odd (7, A3; ☎ 697 4 02 2378; ✉ Marathonos 30, cnr Meg Alexandros, Keramikos)

CINEMAS

Moonlight cinema is one of Athens' summer delights. Outdoor cinemas, which hung on during the threat from video, air-con and multiplexes are enjoying a revival. Unlike most European countries, the Greeks don't dub English-language films. Check listings in the English edition of *Kathimerini* (inside the *International Herald Tribune*) or the *Athens News*.

OUTDOOR CINEMAS

Aigli (7, D6) The oldest outdoor cinema (it used to play silent movies) re-opened in 2000 in the Zappeio Gardens. It has a deal with the restaurant next door for wine and gourmet snack packs during the film or a dinner and movie package.
☎ 210 336 9369 ⌧ Zappeio Gardens € €7 ♿ excellent 🚋 2, 11, 14

Cine Paris (9, D3)
A traditional old rooftop cinema in Plaka with great views of the Acropolis and stereo sound.
☎ 210 322 2071 ⌧ Kydathineon 22, Plaka € €7 Ⓜ Syntagma

Dexameni (6, B2)
Halfway up to Lykavittos Hill, Dexameni has been spruced up, with deck chairs, two bars, Dolby SR, table seating and a gorgeous wall of bougainvillea.

☎ 210 362 3942 ⌧ Plateia Dexameni, Kolonaki € €7 Ⓜ Evangelismos

Thisseion (9, A2) Across from the Acropolis, this is a lovely old-style cinema with a snack bar and garden setting. Sit towards the back if you want to catch a glimpse of the glowing edifice.
☎ 210 342 0864 ⌧ Apostolou Pavlou 7, Thisio € €6.50 ☯ check listings Ⓜ Thisio

INDOOR CINEMAS

Apollon & Attikon Renault (7, D4) This beautifully renovated historic 1960s theatre has the latest screen-and-sound technology and operates year-round.
☎ 210 323 6811 ⌧ Stadiou 19, Syntagma € €7 Ⓜ Panepistimio; Syntagma

Asty (7, D4) A favourite for avant-garde moviegoers,

Catch the latest movies at Aigli cinema

this old theatre has plenty of character and screens arthouse movies.
☎ 210 322 1925 ⌧ Korao 4, Syntagma € €6 (closed summer) Ⓜ Panepistimio

Petit Palai-Filmcentre 2000 (7, F6) The deceptive modern foyer in what looks like a normal apartment block hides a huge, quirky arthouse cinema with balcony and old-style bar.
☎ 210 729 1800 ⌧ cnr Rizari & Hironos, Pangrati € €6.50 (closed summer) Ⓜ Evangelismos

Village Park Renti (1, A2) A 20-cinema entertainment complex in Athens' western suburbs run by the Australian cinema chain.
☎ 210 427 8600 ⌧ Thivon & Petrou Ralli, Renti € €7 🚋 21 from Pireos 🚌 A18, B18 (from Menandrou)

Premiere Nights

Launched in 1995, the annual Athens film festival, **Premiere Nights** (☎ 210 606 1413; www.aiff.gr), screens an eclectic selection of international and Greek independent cinema.

Held in September at the refurbished Apollon and Attikon Renault cinemas, it is organised by movie magazine *Cinema*, in conjunction with the Municipality of Athens.

GAY & LESBIAN ATHENS

The gay scene seems to be gaining momentum and prominence in Athens, with several bars and clubs operating around town, concentrated in Kolonaki and Makrigianni. A new breed of stylish, gay-friendly clubs has seen the younger gay and lesbian scene move to Gazi.

Alekos' Island (6, B2)
One of Athens' original gay bars, run by an artist whose works adorn the walls. It's a candlelit lounge-style hang-out – Alekos even bakes the cakes. Attracts an older bear crowd.
☎ 210 723 9163
✉ Tsakalof 42, Kolonaki
🕑 6pm-late
Ⓜ Syntagma

Aroma Gynekas (7, D2)
The most popular lesbian dance club in Athens plays mainstream and Greek music and is packed on weekends. Check for cyberdykes parties around Athens and the island where it all began, Lesvos (www.lesbian.gr).
☎ 210 381 9615
✉ Tsamadou 15, Exarhia
🕑 10.30pm-late
Ⓜ Omonia

Cone (8, B2) A small club with pop and Greek music that pumps late into the night. It has a more mature crowd than nearby Sodade.
☎ 210 345 8118
✉ Triptolemou 35, Gazi
€ €7.50 🕑 11.30pm-late Ⓜ Thisio 🚕 taxi

Granazi (7, C7) A classic old-style gay haunt on the eastern side of Syngrou that attracts a mature crowd, as does The Guys bar just down the road. It's been going 20 years and plays mainstream music until

> ## Gay Beaches
> The most popular gay beach is **Limanakia**, below the rocky coves of Varkiza, which is part-nudist (as in parts of the beach). Take bus A2 (summer: express E2) from Athens Academy on Panepistimiou or tram A2 to Glyfada, then 115 or 116 to Limanakia B stop.

1pm, Greek after that.
☎ 210 924 4185
✉ Lembesi 20, Makrigianni 🕑 11pm-late (closed Tue) Ⓜ Akropoli

Kirkis & Lizard (8, D3)
A popular gay and lesbian *steki* (hang-out), Kirkis café has a good range of meze for lunch and dinner. The Lizard club upstairs has Acropolis views and a (relatively) quiet lounge area, diverse music and young, friendly crowd.
☎ 210 346 6960
✉ Apostolou Pavlou 31, Thisio 🕑 10am-3am (Lizard 11pm-late Fri-Sun) Ⓜ Thisio

Lamda Club (7, C7)
After 2am, this three-level club is one of the busiest in Athens, attracting a diverse crowd. Pop, house and Greek music dominate, with videos in two basement back rooms and a tropical aquarium

behind the dance floor.
☎ 210 942 4202 ✉ Lembesi 15, (cnr Syngrou), Makrigianni 🕑 closed Aug Ⓜ Akropoli

Mayo Bar (8, B2) One of the newer gay-friendly bars in Gazi, with a great rooftop terrace, quiet mezzanine level courtyard and friendly, casual atmosphere.
☎ 210 342 3066
✉ Persefonis 33, Gazi
🕑 9pm-late Ⓜ Thisio
🚕 taxi

Sodade (8, C1) Gazi's post-industrial theme continues inside this progressive funky venue that plays the latest dance music. Sodade attracts a stylish, under-25s gay-friendly crowd.
☎ 210 346 8657
🖥 www.sodade.gr
✉ Triptolemou 10, Gazi
🕑 11pm-late € €7.50
Ⓜ Thisio 🚕 taxi

> ## Insider Info
> For news on the gay entertainment scene, look out for the *Deon* freezine in clubs or the *Greek Gay Guide* at newsstands (€15) or see websites (p116).

SPORTS

Most major sporting venues in Athens are being upgraded for the Olympics and will reopen in spring 2004. Post-Olympics, the city will be left with world-class sports stadiums. In the meantime, visitors wanting to catch some sport are advised to contact the clubs or sporting bodies direct for venue and match information or check the English-language press.

The Greek Secretariat for Sport has a website (www.sport.gov.gr) with information on all sports organisations and stadiums.

Soccer

Soccer is the most popular sport in Greece and there are three teams in the European's Champions league. Greece's top three teams are Panathinaikos, AEK and Olympiakos. Generally, tickets to major games can be bought on the day at the venue itself. Big games take place at the Olympic Stadium in Maroussi (Ⓜ Irini) and the Karaiskaki stadium in Piraeus (Ⓜ Faliro).

Basketball

Greeks are also keen basketball fans and the biggest games take place at the **Stadium of Peace and Friendship** (5, F2; ☎ 210 489 3000; Ethnarhou Makariou; Ⓜ Faliro) in Palio Faliro. Greek basketball is dominated by Piraeus-based Olympiakos, which did well in the European championships in the early '90s. Greece fields six teams in the Euro League.

Athletics

The annual Tsiklitiria Athens Grand Prix takes place in the summer. Tickets and information are available at www.tsiklitiria.org. The annual Athens Marathon, held in November, attracts thousands of international runners to a course that retraces the steps of the original marathon (p18).

Horse Racing

The new Markopoulo Olympic Equestrian Centre (☎ 2299 081 000) has given Athens a superb racing venue. Race meetings are held on Mondays, Wednesdays and Fridays at 3pm.

Mont Parnes Casino

The **casino** (1, B1; ☎ 210 246 9111; Parnitha; ☼ 4pm-4am, will be 24 hours; 🚍 taxi) on top of Mt Parnes is undergoing a major facelift since being part-privatised in May 2003. Its location in the Mt Parnitha National Park, 40km outside Athens makes for a pleasant trip, with access by cable car.

Now managed by a consortium led by the Hyatt Regency, the extensive €7.3 million refurbishment and extension will turn it into one of Europe's most luxurious casinos, with up to 110 table games and 1500 slot machines, five-star hotel, fitness centre and spa, indoor and outdoor swimming pools, retail shops, conference centre, restaurants and bars. A shuttle bus service from the city was in the pipeline.

Sleeping

Athens has many fine, established hotels for business and leisure travellers, from grand former palaces to contemporary international hotels and smaller family-run affairs. The city's accommodation industry has undergone a major shake-up for the 2004 Olympics. Several new hotels have opened, many older ones have been spruced up, and more than 10,000 new beds have been created. The quality of accommodation has significantly improved, but prices have soared accordingly.

Overall, the industry is becoming more professional and customer-oriented (although there is still some way to go on that one).

Greece's hotel rating method is in the process of changing to the five-star international system, bringing classifications into line with accepted standards. The current classification system is controlled by the Greek National Tourism Organisation (GNTO, or EOT in Greek), which obligates hotels to post official rates on the back of the hotel room door.

> ### Room Rates
>
> The categories listed here are based on the official rack rate quoted per night for a standard double room (although these are often much higher than you would normally pay and moves many hotels up a category). Hotels have also been judged on location and proximity to the centre and main tourist attractions.
>
> | | |
> |---|---|
> | Deluxe | from €390 |
> | Top End | €221–389 |
> | Mid-Range | €81–220 |
> | Budget | under €80 |

The official EOT categories are: L for Luxury and A, B, C, D, E for first to fifth class. Staff in the top categories are expected to speak several languages. Many of Athens' hotels that have these top ratings and price may be disappointing compared with their international counterparts.

Official prices are often much more expensive compared with what you will pay if you haggle or book through an agency (especially during off-peak periods). As prices vary greatly according to season and availability, check with hotels for special rates – and try to negotiate a better deal.

The truly grand hotel Grand Bretagne, complete with 24-hour butler service

DELUXE

Andromeda (6, E1) A member of Small Luxury Hotels of the World, this boutique hotel is in a quiet, tree-lined street behind the Athens Concert Hall and the US embassy. Stylish and intimate, it has all the mod cons on a smaller scale. The rooms are small but comfortable and the service excellent. There are 12 executive apartments across the street.
☎ 210 641 5000
🖥 www.andromeda athens.gr ✉ Timoleontos Vassou 22, Ambelokipi Ⓜ Ambelokipi ✗ Etrusco

Athenaeum Intercontinental (7, A9) An international-standard, ultra-modern hotel with impeccable service, spacious rooms and a marble lobby boasting some serious art. There are Acropolis views from some rooms, a 24-hour health club, big pool and VIP club and there's a great seafood buffet at the rooftop restaurant. Top security makes it the choice for visiting dignitaries.

Galaxy Bar, Athens Hilton: the view comes free

☎ 210 920 6000
🖥 www.intercontinental .com ✉ Syngrou 89-93, Neos Kosmos 🚗 taxi ✗ Café Zoe ♿

Athens Hilton (6, D3) Extensive renovations that closed the hotel for almost a year have restored the Athens landmark to its former status as one of the city's premier hotels. The lavish top-to-bottom redesign is sleek and modern, if a little cold. The panoramic views from the top-level Galaxy Bar (and many rooms) are outstanding. There's a pool, gym and spa.

☎ 210 728 1000
🖥 reservations.athens@ hilton.com ✉ Vassilisis Sofias 46, Athens Ⓜ Evangelismos ♿ good ✗ Byzantino

Divani Caravel (6, D3) Close to the National Gallery and only a short walk from many museums, the Caravel isn't as ostentatious as its rivals but is favoured by business travellers for its good service and hosts many conferences. There's an outdoor pool (heated and covered in winter), roof garden and fitness centre.
☎ 210 720 7000
🖥 www.divanicaravel.gr ✉ Vassileos Alexandrou 2, Ilissia Ⓜ Evangelismos ✗ Millennium ♿

Grand Bretagne (9, F1) The historic, super-exclusive Grande Bretagne reopened in 2003 after a complete renovation, resulting in an even grander hotel. Oozing with opulence, the former palace wins hands down for history, prestige and location,

Under Construction

Many new hotels and refurbished older hotels will be opening in spring 2004 in time for the Olympics. The historic **King George II** (9, F1; ☎ 210 728 0350; www.lhw.com/kinggeorge; Syntagma Sq) looks set to become the top boutique hotel, with a royal suite taking one level (with private pool), and a Leading Hotels of the World stamp. Other promising facelifts include the Iris in Makrigianni and the Athenian Inn in Kolonaki.

let alone its added extras like 24-hour butlers. There's a great rooftop terrace, with restaurant, bar and pool.
☎ 210 333 0000
💻 www.grande bretagne.gr ✉ Vassileos Georgiou 1, Syntagma Sq Ⓜ Syntagma ♿ good ✕ GB Corner ♨

Holiday Suites (6, D3)
Aimed at executive travellers, the spacious suites have faxes, three telephone lines plus data lines to cover any business need as well as home comforts like DVD players and kitchenettes. There is a fitness centre, pool and sauna and access to nearby Holiday Inn facilities. It's all there and reflected in the price.
☎ 210 727 8690
💻 www.holidaysuites.gr ✉ Arnis 4, Ilissia Ⓜ Megaron Mousikis ♿ good ✕ Boschetto (p73)

Margi Hotel (1, B3) An exquisite, boutique hotel

Grand Bretagne's friendly reception

where the personal touch of the owners (two sisters) extends from antiques, handmade furniture and decorative items collected on their travels, to CD players and cordless phones in the rooms. The suites are divine. If you don't need to be in town, the Margi is right next to the beach, with a great pool bar and fine restaurant.
☎ 210 896 2061
💻 www.themargi.gr ✉ Litous 11, Vouliagmeni 🚌 taxi ♿ excellent ✕ Café Tabac

Pentelikon (3, C1) One of the most decadent options in Athens, the exclusive Pentelikon is in a neoclassical mansion in leafy Kifissia, with swimming pool, manicured garden and beautifully furnished rooms. Faultless service, a luxury old world style and a Michelin-rated restaurant make it a real treat.
☎ 210 623 0650-6
💻 www.hotel pentelikon.gr ✉ Deligianni 66, Kefalari 🚌 taxi ✕ Vardis (p80)

Theoxenia Palace (3, C1)
Old-world elegance and modern-city comforts come in a fine location, opposite Kefalari Park in Kifissia. The hotel has stylish and light rooms, conference facilities, and a state-of-the-art gym that looks out onto the outdoor pool.
☎ 210 623 3622-6
💻 www.theoxeniapal ace .com ✉ Filadelfeos 2 (cnr Kolokotroni), Kefalari 🚌 taxi ✕ ♨

TOP END

Athenian Callirhoe (7, C7)
An ultra-chic new boutique hotel catering to the style-conscious, with comfortable rooms and excellent facilities. It is on a major thoroughfare but handy nonetheless. The rooftop restaurant has great views.
☎ 210 921 5353
💻 www.tac.gr ✉ Kallirrois 32, Makrigianni Ⓜ Syngrou-Fix ✕ Chic

Electra Palace (9, E2)
Totally refurbished in 2003, the Electra Palace is in an excellent location in Plaka, with many rooms boasting balconies overlooking the Acropolis – and tables for you take in the view over breakfast or a drink (although the best views are from the roof garden). It has a formal, grand feel throughout, with comfortable, well-appointed rooms.
☎ 210 337 0000,

210 324 1401
💻 www.electrahotels.gr ✉ Navarhou Nikodimou 18, Plaka Ⓜ Syntagma ✕ Daphne's (p75)

Herodion (7, C7) Good service and comfortable, modern rooms make this hotel a pleasant place to stay, centrally located right near the Theatre of Herodes Atticus (after which it is named). There's a rooftop terrace with Parthenon views and a shady courtyard.

☎ 210 923 6832-6
🖥 www.herodion.gr
✉ Rovertou Galli 4, Makrigianni Ⓜ Akropoli Ⓧ Strofi (p69) ♿

Kefalari Suites (3, C1) A stylish hotel in the heart of Kifissia, Kefalari is one for the discerning traveller, with elegant, themed rooms (from French chateau to African Queen) all with kitchenettes. It's not in town, but there are plenty of good restaurants nearby.

☎ 210 623 3333;
🖥 www.kefalarisuites .gr ✉ Pentelis 1 (cnr Kolokotroni), Kifissia 🚌 taxi Ⓧ Ta Kioupia (p80)

NJV Athens Plaza (9, F1) A more contemporary alternative on Syntagma Sq, the Plaza is central, stylish, efficient and comfortable with all the trappings of a five-star hotel, including a fine bar. A family plan allows children under 12 to stay with their parents free.

☎ 210 325 5301-9
🖥 www.grecotelcity.gr
✉ Vassileos Georgiou 2, Syntagma Sq Ⓜ Syntagma Ⓧ Parliament ♿

Athens Acropol (7, C3) Reputedly the capital's funkiest hotel, the refurbished Acropol is certainly trying to attract a more hip, younger clientele to the gritty Omonia area, which is undergoing yet another major face-lift. Apart from the out-there pop art foyer, it has business facilities, ultra-modern rooms and a creative restaurant menu.

☎ 210 528 2100
🖥 www.grecotelcity.gr
✉ Pireos 1, Omonia Sq Ⓜ Omonia Ⓧ Pireos 1

Parthenon (9, D3) Located at the foot of the Acropolis, close to Plaka, this hotel is geared towards the business traveller, but makes an ideal base for checking out the nearby archaeological sites. It has comfortable, clean recently-renovated rooms, many with balconies and views.

☎ 210 923 4594-8
🖥 www.airotel-hotels .com ✉ Makri 6, Makrigianni Ⓜ Akropoli ♿

St George Lycabettus (6, B2) This delightful historic hotel at the foot of pine-clad Lykavittos Hill has great views of the city and an impressive art collection. Rooms are modern, stylish and well appointed, and the lavish suites have accommodated royalty. There's a rooftop pool and bar and two restaurants. The uphill hike is the only catch.

☎ 210 729 0711-9
🖥 www.sglycabettus.gr
✉ Kleomenous 2, Plateia Dexameni, Kolonaki Ⓜ Evangelismos Ⓧ Le Grand Balcon

MID-RANGE

Achilleas (7,C5) Modern and simple, this small, centrally located hotel is in a side street off busy Syntagma Sq. With all the basics, including minibar, air-conditioning and TV, it offers good value for money.

☎ 210 3222 707
🖥 achilleas@tourhotel.gr
✉ Leka 21, Syntagma Ⓜ Syntagma

Acropolis View (7, B7) There are indeed views of the Acropolis from many of the rooms, although the best are from the roof terrace. Other rooms look over Filopappos Hill. A quiet, basic place to stay near the Theatre of Herodes Atticus.

☎ 210 921 7303
🖥 www.acropolis view.gr ✉ Webster 10 (off Rovertou Galli), Makrigianni Ⓜ Akropoli

Alexandros (6, E1) A small luxury hotel popular with business travellers, Alexandros has spacious rooms, excellent facilities and a pleasant, contemporary design. The upper floors have generous balconies with views over the city. Pets can be accommodated.

☎ 210 643 0464
🖥 www.airotel.gr
✉ Timoleontos Vassou 8, Plateia Mavili, Ambelokipi Ⓜ Megaro Moussikis Ⓧ Don Giovanni

Amalia (7, D6) Opposite the National Gardens, and near Plaka, the Amalia is

Children & Pets

Most top hotels can provide babysitting services if given prior notice. Make the request when booking or at least a day before you need one. Hotels offering this service have special arrangements with registered childcare providers. Rates start from €10 per hour and increase after midnight (including paying for a taxi after midnight). A surprising number of Athens' hotels will accommodate pets (with prior notice). Check with individual hotels.

a large hotel with good facilities, a roof garden and lobby café, making it great value for the price.
☎ 210 323 7301-9
🖳 www.amalia.gr
✉ Vas Amalias 10, Syntagma Ⓜ Syntagma 🍴 Aigli (p78)

Coral (1, B3) Right on the water at Palio Faliro, this is a reasonable option, with the new tram taking you into town and its close proximity to Piraeus. The top rooms have verandas and there are modern furnishings throughout, as well as a small gym and pool.
☎ 210 981 6441
🖳 info@coralhotel.gr
✉ Poseidonos 35, Palio Faliro 🚊 A1 🍴 Tselementes (p80)

Esperia Palace (7, D4) It's not much to look at from the street, but the Esperia has been tastefully renovated inside, with good facilities and functional simple rooms. It's in a handy location, just a short walk from Syntagma.
☎ 210 323 8001-9
🖳 www.esperiahotel

.com ✉ Stadiou 22, Syntagma Ⓜ Panepistimio; Syntagma 🍴 Palia Vouli

Hotel Cypria (7, C5) A small hotel in the heart of town, the Cypria offers excellent value, comfort and convenience just off the Ermou shopping precinct. Rooms have a minibar and room service. Adjoining family rooms, cribs and discounts for children make this a good option for families.
☎ 210 323 8034-8
🖳 www.athens cypria.com ✉ Diomias 5, Syntagma Ⓜ Syntagma

Metropolitan (5, F1) A major refurbishment has made this one of the more contemporary hotels in Athens, with excellent business and conference facilities and efficient service. Its location is the biggest drawback, but it is close to the new Faliron coastal zone and port of Piraeus and has an outdoor pool and roof garden.
☎ 210 947 1000
🖳 www.chandris.gr

✉ Syngrou 385, Palio Faliro 🚖 taxi 🍴 Trocadero

Philippos Hotel (7, C7) A great mid-range hotel near the Acropolis, Philippos has a good reputation for service and is popular with business and leisure travellers. The rooms are not as impressively appointed as the lobby and public areas but are comfortable and have all you need.
☎ 210 922 3611 🖳 www .philipposhotel.gr
✉ Mitseon 3, Makrigianni Ⓜ Akropoli ♿

Titania (7, C3) The 400-room Titania has been renovated and given a significant face-lift. It is a comfortable, modern hotel with large rooms and good facilities for the price, although it is on a busy street. There are great views over the city at night from the rooftop piano bar (and the 8th and 9th floor rooms) and the restaurant is well recommended.
☎ 210 330 0111
🖳 www.titania.gr
✉ Panepistimiou 52, Omonia Ⓜ Omonia; Panepistimio 🍴 Olive Garden ♿

BUDGET

Acropolis House (9, E2)
An old pension in a 19th-century Plaka residence favoured by artists and academics, this family-run hotel has 20 large but basic rooms with original frescoes, clean, simple décor and friendly owners. Some rooms have their own bathrooms just outside in the hallway, but not all have air-con. A little outdated but full of character.
☎ 210 322 2344; fax 210 324 4143 ✉ Kodrou 6-8, Plaka Ⓜ Syntagma

Cecil Hotel (7, B4) This fine old family-run hotel was recently renovated, making it a charming, good-value place to stay. It has polished timber floors, high moulded ceilings and 36 tastefully furnished rooms with TV, air-con and minibar. Soundproofing is planned but in the meantime get a room at the back.
☎ 210 321 7079 ▢ www.cecil-hotel.com ✉ Athinas 39, Monastiraki Ⓜ Monastiraki

Acropolis House; not as grand as the Acropolis

Dorian Inn (7, B3)
Uninspiring on the outside, the Dorian is nonetheless a central, standard hotel on busy Pireos with reasonably-priced, clean, comfortable rooms and suites, a restaurant and bar, plus a small rooftop pool with views of the Acropolis and Lykavittos.
☎ 210 523 9782 ▢ www.greekhotel.com /athens/dorianinn ✉ Pireos 15-17, Omonia Ⓜ Omonia ✕ Athina-ikon (p74)

Erechtion (9, A2) The revitalisation of the Thisio area, with the major pedestrianisation programme around the Acropolis, has boosted the appeal of the area's budget hotels, now among the quietest in Athens. The Erechtion is close to all the cafés, eateries and sites and has views from most rooms.
☎ 210 345 9606; fax 210 345 9626 ✉ Flammarion 8, Thisio Ⓜ Thisio ✕ Filistron (p69)

Hotel Exarchion (7, D3)
For a lively neighbourhood experience, this cheap, though dated hotel is right at the heart of Exarhia's student and café-bar scene. Rooms are basic but clean, with air-con and TV. There's a rooftop café-bar from which you can watch the action, washing facilities and an Internet café in the foyer.
☎ 210 380 0731; fax 210 380 3296 ✉ Themistokleous 55, Exarhia Ⓜ Omonia ✕ Cookou Food (p70)

Marble House Pension (7, B8) A little further afield from the centre (but near the metro), this charming guesthouse is popular with budget travellers because of its friendly reputation and excellent value. The rooms are simple and comfortable and there is a pleasant courtyard.
☎ 210 923 4058 ▢ www.marble.house .gr ✉ Zini 35, Koukaki Ⓜ Syngrou-Fix

Plaka Hotel (9, C1)
A value-for-money hotel central to Plaka, Monastiraki and the Ermou shopping strip, making it a great base. The recently-renovated rooms are comfortable and spacious and there is a quiet rooftop garden with great views.
☎ 210 322 2096 ▢ www.plakahotel.gr ✉ Kapnikareas 7 (cnr Mitropoleos) Ⓜ Monastiraki

Tempi Hotel (7, C5) A super no-frills hotel in the pleasant pedestrian stretch of Eolou, opposite a church, the Tempi is a friendly family-run place with simple, clean rooms, many with private bathrooms (some shared). There is a communal fridge and tea and coffee facilities. It's cheap but not nasty.
☎ 210 321 3175 ▢ www.travelling.gr/ tempihotel ✉ Eolou 29, Athens Ⓜ Monastiraki ✕ Aeolis

About Athens

HISTORY
Ancient Athens

The Acropolis drew some of Greece's earliest Neolithic settlers. By 1400 BC, it had become a powerful Mycenaean city whose territory covered most of Attica. By the end of the 7th century BC, Athens had become the artistic centre of Greece.

Athens was ruled by aristocrats and tyrants until Solon, the harbinger of democracy, became *arhon* (chief magistrate) in 594 BC and declared all free Athenians equal by law. He introduced sweeping social and economic reforms that led to Athens becoming the cradle of European civilisation and democracy.

In 490 BC, the Persian army reached Attica but were humiliatingly defeated when outmanoeuvred in the Battle of Marathon. They returned in 480 BC, and virtually burned Athens to the ground.

Mycenaean gold jewellery

Classical Age

Under Pericles' leadership (461–429 BC), the treasury moved from Delos to Athens and an illustrious rebuilding programme began. Athens experienced a golden age of unprecedented cultural, artistic and scientific achievement.

However Athens' expansionist ambitions eventually sparked the Peloponnesian Wars, in which Athens suffered badly. During the first war (431–421 BC) a plague broke out in the city, killing a third of the population, including Pericles. After Athens surrendered to Sparta in the second war, its fleet was confiscated and the Delian League, the alliance of Greek city-states formed to defend against the Persians, was abolished.

Hellenistic Period

The northern kingdom of Macedon led by Philip II emerged as the new power in 338 BC. After Philip's assassination, his son Alexander (the Great) became king and by the end of the 3rd century BC had spread Hellenism into Persia, Egypt and parts of India and Afghanistan. Alexander treated Athens favourably. His tutor Aristotle taught at the Athens Lyceum. But an unsuccessful bid for independence after Alexander's death led to an intermittent period of subjection to Macedon, although the city's institutions were upheld.

Roman Rule

Athens was defeated by Rome in 189 BC after it backed an enemy of Rome in Asia Minor, but the city escaped lightly as the Romans had great respect for Athenian scholarship and supported the teachings of Athenian philosophers. After a second ill-fated rebellion, the Romans destroyed the city walls and carted off many of its finest statues to Rome.

Athens received a pardon from Julius Caesar and, for the next 300 years, it experienced an unprecedented period of peace – the Pax Romana – and became the seat of learning, attracting the sons of rich Romans. During this period Roman emperors, particularly Hadrian, graced Athens with many grand buildings.

Byzantine Empire

Byzantine Church of the Holy Apostles

With the rise of the Byzantine Empire, which blended Hellenistic culture with Christianity, the Greek city of Byzantium (renamed Constantinople in AD330, present-day Istanbul) became the capital of the Roman Empire.

The Byzantine Empire outlived Rome, lasting until the Turks captured Constantinople in 1453. Christianity was made the official religion of Greece in 394, and worship of Greek and Roman gods was banned.

Athens remained an important cultural centre until 529, when the teaching of 'pagan' classical philosophy was forbidden in favour of Christian theology. From 1200 to 1450, Athens was occupied by a succession of opportunistic invaders – Franks, Catalans, Florentines and Venetians.

Ottoman Rule

In 1456 Athens was captured by the Turks, who ruled Greece for the next 400 years. The Acropolis became the home of the Ottoman governor, the Parthenon was converted into a mosque and the Erechtheion was used as a harem. Athens enjoyed a privileged administrative status and a period of relative peace ensued, with some economic prosperity from trade, particularly with the Venetians. Conflict between the Turks and Venetians led the Venetian general Morosini to lay siege to the Acropolis for two months in 1687, briefly interrupting Turkish control of the city. It was during this campaign that the Parthenon was blown up when Venetian artillery struck gunpowder stored inside the temple.

Independence

On 25 March 1821, the Greeks launched the War of Independence and on 13 January 1822 independence was declared. But infighting twice escalated into civil war, allowing the Ottomans to recapture Athens, whereupon the Western powers stepped in and destroyed the Turkish-Egyptian fleet in the Bay of Navarino.

In April 1827 Ioannis Kapodistrias was elected president, and the city of Nafplio named the capital. After Kapodistrias was assassinated in 1831, Britain, France and Russia again intervened, declaring Greece a monarchy. To avoid taking sides, the throne was given to 17-year-old

Prince Otto of Bavaria, who transferred his court to Athens, which became the capital in 1834.

At the time there were about 6000 residents in Athens, many having fled after Athens suffered in the siege of 1827. King Otto (as he became) brought in Bavarian architects to create a city of imposing neoclassical buildings, tree-lined boulevards, flower gardens and squares. Sadly, many of these building have been demolished.

World War II & the Greek Civil War

Athens thrived and enjoyed a brief heyday as the 'Paris of the eastern Mediterranean' before WWI. A disastrous Greek attempt to seize former Greek territories in southern Turkey, known as the Asia Minor catastrophe, ended with the Treaty of Lausanne in July 1923.

More than one million Greeks were forced out of Turkey in the ensuing population exchange. Many headed for Athens, virtually doubling the city's population overnight.

During the German occupation of WWII, more Athenians were killed by starvation than by the enemy. After the war, fighting between communist and monarchist resistance groups led to a bitter civil war that ended in October 1949, leaving the country in a political, social and economic mess.

In a mass exodus, almost a million Greeks migrated to the USA, Canada and Australia. A mammoth reconstruction and industrialisation programme in Athens prompted another population boom, as people from the islands and villages moved to the city.

Junta & Monarchy

In 1967, a group of right-wing army colonels (the junta) launched a military coup. In their ensuing seven-year reign, political parties and trade unions were banned and opponents were jailed or exiled.

On 17 November 1973, tanks stormed a student sit-in at Athens' polytechnic, killing at least 20 students. The US-backed junta's downfall came after the disastrous attempt to topple the Makarios government in Cyprus provoked a Turkish invasion of the island.

Democracy returned to Greece in 1974 and a referendum subsequently abolished the monarchy, which remains in exile today. A dispute between the former king, Constantine, and the government over the family's assets was settled in 2002 and the former royal family now often returns to Greece as private citizens with no privileges (although they remain well connected, with friends in high places).

Athens Today

Since the 1980s, fundamental social and economic changes have taken place as Greece fast-tracked its development into a modern country, with the most dramatic changes occurring in the '90s and the years leading up to the 2004 Olympics. Athens has become a more modern, cosmopolitan and wealthy society over the last 20 years, although there are still high social imbalances, and it is in many ways struggling to keep up with itself.

Greece is fast becoming part of the global economy, with foreign companies making investments and a raft of privatisations bound to change the notorious public sector mentality and bureaucracy. Greece is also becoming a major economic player in the Balkans.

Authorities have embarked on an ambitious programme to modernise the capital. Key infrastructure projects, including expansion of road and transport networks and the new airport, have made Athens a more efficient and functional capital, though it's still a case study in organised chaos. Confidence is high and billions are being poured into city centre redevelopment for the 2004 Olympics; their legacy will be a city transformed.

ENVIRONMENT

Athens' Mediterranean climate means hot, dry summers and mild winters with bright sunny days. In July and August, heat waves can send the mercury soaring above 40°C (over 100°F) for days on end and the city can be unbearably hot. Warm summer nights force people out for relief, contributing to Athens' lively nightlife. It does not rain for months on end in the summer.

Greece is belatedly becoming environment conscious, with campaigns being implemented in schools. An army of road sweepers tackle the litter problem in the city, but rural areas can be a disgrace.

Are trees taking over Athens?

Athens suffers significantly less now from the dreaded *nefos*, the blanket of smog that still covers the city on bad days. Restrictions on vehicles in the centre, better public transport, the gradual abolition of leaded petrol and tougher laws have reduced vehicle and industrial pollution.

A major programme to increase green space was to see more than one billion trees, shrubs and plants planted in the Attica area by 2004. Forest fires remain a major problem throughout Greece.

GOVERNMENT & POLITICS

Since 1975 Greece has been a parliamentary republic with a president as head of state. The president and 300-member parliament have joint legislative power. The left-wing PASOK government of Andreas Papandreou was elected in 1981, the same year Greece entered the EU.

Apart from a brief comeback by the conservative New Democracy party in 1990–93, PASOK has been in power for nearly 20 years. Prime Minister Costas Simitis was facing an election in early 2004, with the polls predicting a change of government, despite widespread lack of confidence in the opposition. Some pundits suggest a change of government is unlikely so close to the Olympics (August 2004).

Athens is part of the prefecture *(nomos)* of Attica. In 2002, former New Democracy MP Dora Bakoyianni, daughter of former prime minister Konstantine Mitsotakis, was elected mayor of Athens, the first woman to

Diaspora

Greece maintains strong links with more than four million Greeks living around the world, including an estimated two million in the US and Canada. Many return for annual holidays, own property and are involved in the political and cultural life of the country of their birth (or their ancestors').

The Greek government has a significant commitment to promoting Greek language, culture and religion abroad and has established a dedicated General Secretariat for Greeks Abroad. Melbourne, Australia, has the third-largest population of Greek-speakers in the world, after Athens and Thessaloniki.

hold the post. She is overseeing the major public works programme begun by her predecessor Dimitris Avramopoulos. The beautification of the city's streets, buildings and squares, and the unification of archaeological sites in a pedestrian precinct, has revitalised the centre of town.

Once the black sheep of the EU, Athens has gained respect for its leadership role in the Balkans and in 2003 successfully held the six-month rotating presidency of the EU during the sensitive Iraq war period.

During the Greek presidency, Cyprus was admitted to the EU, although a settlement on the island's division has yet to be reached. Relations with Turkey remain sensitive but a climate of common cause has led to much economic cooperation and hope for a resolution to the Cyprus issue.

ECONOMY

Greece's entry to the European Monetary Union in January 2002 was a momentous achievement. The drachma was phased out from February 2002 to make way for the euro.

Tighter fiscal policy, structural reforms and a recent programme of deregulation and privatisation of the telecommunications, electricity, shipping and airline industries have improved Greece's economy.

GDP has been growing by 3.5% per annum; growth was expected to reach 4% in 2004, the highest rate in the EU, though spiralling public debt and budget deficits due to

Did you Know?

Athens population: 3.7 million
Inflation rate: 3.5%
Greek GDP per capita: US$19,000
Unemployment: 9%
Number of Greeks outside Greece: 4 million
Number of tourists in Greece in 2002: 14.1 million

Olympics-related development are causing concern. Tourism is the biggest industry, and the majority of the workforce is employed in services (69% of GDP) and industry (23%), with agriculture contributing only 8%.

Unemployment is still high (9%) but inflation is being contained after dropping from 20% in 1990 to 3.5% in late 2003. The 2001 census estimated Athens' population at 3.7 million, including more than 600,000 immigrants (Greece's population was 10.6 million).

Greece's economic prospects have never been brighter. A late-'90s stockmarket frenzy made many rich, but many ordinary punters lost out in the ensuing crash, from which the Bourse is still recovering.

There has been an outcry over widespread price rises since the introduction of the euro. Athens is one of the most expensive European cities, despite wages being among the EU's lowest. The inexplicable disparity between wages and spending suggests the black economy is still going strong.

SOCIETY & CULTURE

Although there are Athenians of several generations' standing, a large proportion of residents today are relative newcomers to the city, who migrated from other parts of Greece or from Greek communities around the world. Many are descended from families forced out of the Smyrna (now Izmir) region of Turkey in 1923, or who arrived in the 1950s from rural areas during the country's comparatively belated entry into the industrial era.

> ### Dos & Don'ts
>
> The Greek reputation for hospitality is not a myth, just a bit harder to find these days in a big and self-absorbed city. Greeks are generous hosts, and guests are expected to contribute nothing to a meal or social gathering. If you are invited out for a meal, the bill is not shared – insisting can insult your host.
>
> Personal questions are not considered rude in Greece, and queries about your age, salary and marital status are considered normal, and opinions expressed freely.

Many Athenians still retain a strong link to their village or island of origin, returning periodically during holidays and on weekends to see parents and grandparents, or to use family properties as holiday homes.

Greece, which lost much of its population to mass migration, is now attracting large numbers of migrants, both legal and illegal, including Albanians and refugees from the Balkans, the former Soviet Union, Bangladesh, Pakistan, Iran and Iraq. Immigration is changing the social and economic landscape and forcing Greek society to confront new social issues.

The city's increasing cultural diversity is becoming apparent in downtown Athens, which has an emerging mini Chinatown, Pakistani hairdressers, Asian food stores and areas where clusters of minorities meet. The growing number of ethnic restaurants reflects both the new communities in Athens and an increasing interest in other cuisines.

But Greece remains largely culturally homogeneous and steeped in traditional customs. Name days (celebrating the saint after whom a person is named) are more important than birthdays and come with an open-house policy where you are expected to feed all well-wishers. Weddings and funerals are also events of great significance in Greek society. Greeks are superstitious and believe in the 'evil eye' (bad luck brought on by envy; for more information see p66), so avoid being too complimentary about things of beauty, especially newborn babies.

About 98% of the Greek population belong to the Greek Orthodox Church, though this will change given migrants make up nearly a tenth of the country's population. Most of the remainder are Roman Catholic, Jewish or Muslim. Religion remains an important criterion in defining what it is to be a Greek, as the controversy over the removal of religion from the state-issued ID card proved. Furthermore, the Greek year is centred around the festivals of the church calendar.

The younger generations of Greeks are highly literate, with a large number studying abroad. A high proportion speak English and are in tune with world trends, fashion and music.

ARTS

The artistic legacy of ancient Greece remains unsurpassed, and is an enduring influence on Western civilisation. People still read Homer's *Iliad* and *Odyssey*, written in 9th century BC, and ancient sculptures take pride of place in the collections of the world's great museums. Generations of artists have been influenced by the ancient Greeks, from primitive and powerful forms of prehistoric art to the realism of the Hellenistic period that inspired Michelangelo.

Architecture

The influence of ancient Greek architecture can be seen today in buildings from Washington, DC to Melbourne. Greek temples, seen throughout history as symbols of democracy, have been the inspiration for major architectural movements such as the Italian Renaissance and the British Greek Revival.

One of the earliest known examples of Greek architecture is the huge Minoan palace complex at Knossos on Crete.

In the archaic and classical periods, monumental temples were characterised by Doric, Ionic and Corinthian columns – the Temple of Athena Nike and the Erechtheion on the Acropolis are two examples. The distinct and ornate Corinthian column features a single or double row of leafy scrolls, later used by the Romans, notably on the Temple of Olympian Zeus.

During the Hellenistic period, private houses and palaces, rather than temples and public buildings, were the main focus.

Byzantine churches built throughout Greece usually featured a central dome supported by four arches on piers and flanked by vaults, with smaller domes at the four corners and three apses to the east. The external brickwork, which alternated with stone, was sometimes set in patterns.

After independence, Athens continued the neoclassical style that had been dominant in Western European architecture and sculpture, exemplified by the grandiose National Library and the Athens University.

Many neoclassical buildings were destroyed in the untamed modernisation that took place in the 1950s, '60s and '70s, when most of the ugly concrete apartment blocks that now characterise the modern city were built.

A number of old mansions are now museums and many more are being restored as buildings and have become heritage protected. The wonderful design of the new metro, with art and antiquities, is in stark contrast to the bland German-designed airport, which could be anywhere. Innovative restorations such as the old Gazi gasworks complex and the Athinais Centre, in an old silk factory, are world class.

Cinema

Greek cinema has for many years been associated with the slow, visual feasts of critically acclaimed director Theodoros Angelopoulos, awarded the 1998 Cannes Palme d'Or for *An Eternity and One Day*. Since the mid-'90s, Greek cinema has been experiencing a revival with local audiences, following the domestic commercial success of a number of Greek films. A talented group of contemporary filmmakers is producing some worthy films and making some inroads into the international film festival circuit.

Drama & Theatre

Drama dates back to the contests staged in Athens during the 6th century BC for the annual Dionysia Festival. At one of these contests, Thespis left the ensemble and took centre stage for a solo performance – considered the first true dramatic performance and leading to the term 'thespian'.

A strong theatre tradition continues today, with the works of ancient Greek playwrights such as Aeschylus, Sophocles, Euripides and Aristophanes performed in the few surviving ancient theatres during summer festivals, most notably at Epidauros and the Theatre of Herodes Atticus. The Greek National Theatre, which stages the pre-eminent performances of Ancient Greek theatre, regularly tours internationally and in Greece.

Literature

Pre-eminent ancient poets included Pindar, Sappho and Alcaeus; modern celebrated poets include Constantine Cavafy and Yiannis Ritsos and the two Nobel Prize laureates, George Seferis (1963) and Odysseus Elytis (1979).

The great classical writers included Homer, the historian and anthropologist Herodotus, Plutarch, Pausanias and Thucydides.

The controversial Nikos Kazantzakis, author of *Zorba the Greek* and *The Last Temptation*, remains the most celebrated 20th-century Greek novelist. A spate of translations of modern Greek writers is helping promote the current generation's literary talents internationally.

Music

Music has always been a feature of Greek life, but not many have made it big internationally, the notable exceptions being opera diva Maria Callas, living legend Mikis Theodorakis, composer Manos Hatzidakis, Vangelis, Demis Roussos and Nana Mouskouri. A new generation of musicians, however, is starting to make an impact on the world music scene, including Mario Frangoulis and vocal artist Savina Yannatou. Many revivalist groups are breathing new life into traditional music and a movement towards *entekno* (artistic or quality) music has spawned a talented generation of singer-songwriters.

Directory

The Ancient Greek punishment for rude taxi drivers, Benaki Museum (p16)

ARRIVAL & DEPARTURE
Air

The **Eleftherios Venizelos international airport** (2, D2) opened in March 2001 near Spata, 27km east of Athens, among the vineyards and olive groves of east Attica. Its facilities are radically better than those at the former airport in Hellinikon, although some bemoan its lack of character.

One of the most hi-tech and efficient European airports, it has state-of-the-art security systems as well as cafés, shops and banks. The airport is connected to the city and the ports of Piraeus and Rafina via express buses and the metro (a direct rail link is expected by mid-2004). It is also equipped to deal with special-needs travellers, with lifts for the mobility impaired and even toilets with Braille.

A small museum on the departure level (near Gate 3) displays interesting archaeological finds unearthed during construction of the airport (☽ 6am to 11pm).

INFORMATION
General Inquiries   ☎ 210 357 1037
Flight Information   ☎ 210 353 0000
  (all airlines)
Hotel Booking Service ☎ 210 353 0445-7
  (GNTO Airport Office)
Airport Information Online
                    ⌨ www.aia.gr

AIRPORT ACCESS
Train The suburban rail extension, due to be completed in 2004, will cut travel time considerably. By mid-2004 the metro station Doukissas Plakentias (Line 3) is expected to link the metro with the suburban rail line for an express service to the airport.

At the time of writing, the quickest way to the airport was a combination of train and bus. Take the metro to Ethniki Amina and catch the E94 express airport bus. The trip should take 25 to 35 minutes.

Bus The E95 airport express bus (24 hours) leaves from Vas Amalias (opposite Othonos) in Syntagma, outside the Parliament, every 10 minutes during peak times, and takes about an hour – longer when traffic is bad. Bus E96 connects the airport with Piraeus and leaves from Plateia Karaïskaki in Piraeus. Express buses to the airport can also be taken from the metro stations at Dafni (E97) and Kifissia (E92). The E93 connects with the Peloponnese bus terminal.

Although buses run 24 hours, the metro stops just after midnight. A one-day travel ticket (€2.90), which gets you to or from the airport, is valid for 24 hours on all transport and can be purchased from the airport bus kiosk, metro terminals and transport kiosks around Athens.

Taxi Cabs from the centre take an average of 30 to 40 minutes to get to the airport, longer if traffic congestion is bad. Expect to pay between €15 and €20 (depending on traffic) to or from the city centre, which includes freeway toll and baggage surcharge. Remember, tariffs to the airport are single, unless travel time coincides with tariff changes (see p113).

Bus

Bus travel in Greece is inexpensive, usually comfortable and relatively fast. For information on routes, schedules and tickets call ☎ 185.

International coaches arriving from Turkey, Bulgaria and Albania go to the Peloponnese station, next to the **Larisis railway station** (7, A1; ☎ 210 529 8740).

Terminal A, northwest of Omonia (☎ 210 513 4588, 210 512 4910; Kifissou 100), has buses to the Peloponnese, Ionian Islands and western Greece. Bus 015 runs to the centre (Omonia) from the station, from 5am to midnight.

Terminal B is 5km north of Omonia off Liossion (☎ 210 831 7096; Agios Dimitriou Oplon).

There are buses for most Attica destinations from the **Mavromateon terminal** (☎ 210 821 3203; cnr 28 Oktovriou-Patission & Alexandras). Buses to Rafina and Marathon leave from stops 150m north on Mavromateon.

Train

Eurail (www.eurail.com) and **Inter-Rail** (www.interrailnet.com) passes are valid in Greece, but it's not worth buying one if Greece is the only place you'll use it.

International trains arrive at Larisis station, as do trains from Thessaloniki and the Peloponnese. For ticketing and schedule information call ☎ 210 529 7777 or check www.ose.gr.

The **Greek Railroad Organisation** (OSE) has offices at Sina 6, Syntagma (6, A2; ☎ 210 362 4402-6) and Karolou 1, Omonia (7, B3; ☎ 210 524 0647).

Boat

Piraeus is the busiest port in Greece with a bewildering number of departures and destinations, including daily services to the islands (except the Ionians and the Sporades). Ferries from Italy dock at Patras in the Peloponnese, and Igoumenitsa in northwestern Greece.

FERRY

Weekly ferry schedules, company details and tickets are available from tourist offices, online (www.greekferries.gr or www.gtp.gr) and in the English edition of *Kathimerini* in the *International Herald Tribune*. The main companies are **Minoan Lines** (☎ 210 408 0006-16;

www.ferries.gr/minoan) with Super fast Ferries, and **Blue Star Ferries** (☎ 210 322 6400; www.bluestar ferries.com).

To book a cabin or take a car on board, it is advisable to buy a ticket in advance. Otherwise, there are agents selling tickets in Piraeus (especially around Plateia Karaïskaki). You can also buy tickets on the ferry.

Most ferries heading to the Cycladic, Saronic and Dodecanese Islands and Crete leave from Piraeus or Rafina, although the new port at Lavrio was expected to service Mykonos and other Cycladic islands.

HYDROFOILS/DOLPHINS

Hydrofoil services operate from the main port in Piraeus or Marina Zea and cut travel time by almost half, making them a very convenient way to get to islands. However, strong wind conditions can lead to cancellations. **Hellas Flying Dolphins** (☎ 210 419 9000; ☺ 8am-8pm Mon-Fri, 8am-4pm Sat-Sun) has regular services and takes credit-card bookings. For information and schedules, see www.dolphins.gr (see also Blue Star Ferries above).

Travel Documents
PASSPORT

You need a valid passport to enter Greece (or ID card for EU nationals), which must also be produced when registering in a hotel or pension.

VISA

No visa is required for stays of less than 90 days for nationals from Australia, Canada, EU countries, USA, Israel, Japan, New Zealand, Norway, Switzerland and most South American countries. Others, and those wanting longer stays, should check with their local Greek embassy.

Customs & Duty Free

There are no longer duty-free restrictions within the EU, but random customs searches are still made for drugs. Customs inspections for non-EU tourists are usually cursory, although there are spot checks.

You can bring an unlimited amount of foreign currency and travellers cheques into the country but if you intend to leave with more than US$2000 in cash you must declare the sum upon entry.

Import regulations for medicines are strict. Importing codeine-based medication is illegal without a doctor's certificate. Dogs and cats must have a vet's certificate.

Exporting antiquities (anything over 100 years old) is strictly forbidden without an export permit. It is an offence to remove even the smallest article from an archaeological site.

There are no duty-free sales within the EU. Non-EU residents can bring 200 cigarettes or 50 cigars; 1L of spirits or 2L of wine; 50g of perfume; 250mL of eau de Cologne and gifts with a value of up to €150. Cameras, laptops and video recorders should be declared and a stamp put in your passport, otherwise you may be asked for proof that you did not buy them in Greece.

Left Luggage

Pacific Baggage Storage near Exit 1 in the Arrivals Terminal (☎ 210 353 0352) charges €3 (small), €4.50 (medium) and €6 (large) for a minimum of six hours. Rates change every six hours and after 48 hours there is a daily charge.

Pacific Baggage Storage (9, E1; ☎ 210 324 1007; Nikis 26; ☺ 8am-8pm Mon-Sat, 9am-2pm Sun) in Syntagma, charges €2 per day, €7 per week and €1 for each additional day, regardless of size.

GETTING AROUND

The sparkling new metro system has made getting around the centre of Athens relatively painless, and with the extension of the whole network it should ease the city's notorious traffic congestion. Athens also has an extensive bus and trolley (electric cable bus) network that was being upgraded in the lead up to the 2004 Olympics.

Travel Passes

Daily travel passes (€2.90) for buses, trolleys and the metro (including travel to and from the airport) are valid for 24 hours.

Metro

The metro's coverage is still largely confined to the centre, although several extensions are to be completed by 2007. Many stations have impressive displays of antiquities

and public art, with Syntagma and Evangelismos virtually museums in their own right. Trains run 5am to midnight, every three minutes at peak times, then every 10 minutes.

Three lines make up the network: the old Kifissia–Piraeus ISAP-Line 1 (green line), Line 2 (red line) from Sepolia to Dafni and Line 3 (blue line) Monastiraki to Ethniki Amina. There are transfer stations at Attiki, Omonia (Line 1 and 2), Syntagma and Monastiraki (Line 1 and 3).

Ticket pricing is complicated. Travel on Lines 2 and 3 costs €0.70, while Line 1 is split into three sections: Piraeus to Monastiraki, Monastiraki to Attiki and Attiki to Kifissia (€0.60 one section, €0.70 for two or more). Tickets must be validated at the machines on platform entrances. Tickets are valid for 90 minutes and allow connections with trains going in one direction, but you cannot leave and re-enter the station using the same ticket.

New stations to be ready by June 2004 include Doukissas Plakentias, which will link to the airport express, A Panagoulis on the southbound extension (Line 2) and Agios Antonios to the west.

Tram

More than 25 years after the last tram trundled through Athens, the city is expecting a new tram system to be operating by mid-2004. Initially, there will be two lines, A1 from Syntagma to Neo Faliro and A2 from Syntagma to Glyfada. This 24km route will connect the southern coastal area of Athens with the centre of the city. There will be three interchanges connecting the tram with the metro – at Syngrou-Fix, Neos Kosmos and Faliro; for details visit www.tramsa.gr.

Trolleybuses

Athens' overhead cable trolleybuses run between 5am and midnight. The Greek National Tourist Organisation (GNTO, or EOT in Greek; www.gnto.gr) produces a free map showing most of the routes.

A flat fare of €0.45 covers one journey on a bus or trolley. Purchase tickets at a transport kiosk or at most *periptera* (kiosks). Validate tickets by inserting them in the onboard machines.

Bus

Athens' bus fleet was being updated and increased to cater for the influx of visitors and increased transport needs during the Olympics, including 600 natural gas–powered buses.

Suburban Buses (blue and white) operate every 15 minutes, from 5am to midnight. Timetables can be obtained from the **GNTO** (www.gnto.gr), or the **Athens Urban Transport Organisation** (OASA; www.oasa.gr).

Taxi

Athens' taxis are relatively inexpensive but hailing one can be incredibly frustrating. During busy times, you may have to stand on the pavement and shout your destination as they pass (and they don't always slow down). If a taxi is going your way, the driver may stop even if there are already passengers inside, but this doesn't mean you share the fare. Check the meter when you get in, deduct that amount from the final fare and add the flag fall.

Athens' taxi drivers have a reputation for ripping off tourists and while this is not the norm, exercise some care in case you are unlucky enough to land one of the nasty rogues (beware it is often the friendly ones who are the worst). Many were being put through charm school pre-Olympics and stricter monitoring was expected.

Fees should be displayed in the cab and drivers are being required to provide a receipt on request.

Flag fall is €0.75, with surcharges from ports, railway and bus stations (€0.70), the airport (€2) and for baggage (€0.29 per item over 10kg). The day rate (€0.26 per km) doubles between midnight and 5am (tariff 2). A minimum fare of €1.50 applies.

You can also call a radio taxi (€2.20 extra). Radio taxis in central Athens include: **Athina 1** (☎ 210 921 7942), **Evropi** (☎ 210 502 9764), **Ikaros** (☎ 210 515 2800) and **Kosmos** (☎ 18 300).

Car & Motorcycle

Driving in Athens can be quite daunting and frustrating. Roads are not always well signposted and you don't get much notice of when to turn or change lanes. Unless you're familiar with the city, one-way streets and no-through roads can leave you stranded or going around in circles.

ROAD RULES

Someone once said red lights in Athens were merely a suggestion and this sums up the traffic chaos that can reign in the centre. That said, greater traffic police presence and hefty fines have led to greater enforcement of seat belt, drink driving and speeding laws, although Athenian's legendary creative parking talents are truly impressive. Greeks drive on the right. Seat belts are compulsory in front seats. The minimum driving age is 18. The speed limit in retail and residential areas is 40km/h and 120km/h on highways and motorways. The blood alcohol limit is 0.05%. Use of mobile phones while driving is theoretically banned, although the bizarre sight of people using them while riding mopeds is common.

RENTAL

Car rentals are expensive but you really only need one for excursions out of Athens. Multinationals can charge up to 25% more than local companies. The top of Syngrou, off Vas Amalias, is lined with car-rental firms, including **Avis** (☎ 210 322 4951), **Budget** (☎ 210 921 4771) and **Europcar** (☎ 210 924 8810).

MOTORING ORGANISATIONS

If your vehicle breaks down, the **Greek Automobile Club** (ELPA; 6, F1; ☎ 210 779 1615; Athens Tower, Mesogeion 2-4, Ambelokipi) has a toll-free 24-hour emergency number (☎ 10400). The club offers reciprocal services to members of national automobile associations with a valid membership card.

PRACTICALITIES
Climate & When to Go

Spring and late autumn are the best times to visit. It is pleasantly warm and sunny, the archaeological sites and museums are less crowded, and hotel rooms are easier to find – and cheaper.

In summer, particularly during July and August heat waves, the temperatures can hover around 40°C for days on end. Most Athenians escape to the islands, making it easier to get around. Hotel rooms are expensive and hard to find.

Winter is generally mild and sunny compared to other European capitals, but there is the occasional rainy day and even exceptional cases of snow. The city – along with its social and cultural life – takes on a remarkably different character.

Disabled Travellers

Facilities for the mobility impaired are a recent phenomenon, being fast-tracked for the Paralympics in 2004, when in theory all public buildings should be wheelchair friendly.

Making the rest of the city accessible is a monumental challenge given its difficult terrain.

Many museums have stairs, most archaeological sites are not wheelchair friendly and public transport can be fairly crowded. Modern restaurants may have restrooms that allow easier access, but tavernas and inner-city eateries often have toilets down stairs.

Many hotels have upgraded their facilities, or are in the process

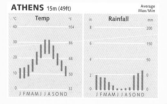

ATHENS 15m (49ft)

of doing so, and quite a few of the better (and therefore more expensive) ones are well equipped.

Newer buses and trolleys are wider and have seats assigned for those with disabilities, but getting on or off is not easy. The new metro has lifts to the platforms. The airport has excellent facilities.

INFORMATION & ORGANISATIONS
The **Panhellenic Union of Paraplegic & Physically Challenged** (1, D2; ☎ 210 483 2564; www.pasipka.gr; Dimetane's 3-5, Moschato) can provide information.

Discounts
Children under 18 and EU students get free admission to state-run museums and archaeological sites (and some private museums), as do students of classics and fine arts from non-EU countries. Families can also get discounts at some museums and galleries.

Some private airlines, such as Aegean, offer discount fares to seniors over 65. Children under 12 pay up to 50% less with some tour companies.

STUDENT & YOUTH CARDS
Students with an International Student Identity Card (ISIC) shouldn't have a problem obtaining discounts to archaeological sites, museums, cinemas and public transport. EU students get free admission to many museums and archaeological sites. Discounts may also apply for domestic and EU flights.

SENIORS' CARDS
Card-carrying EU pensioners can claim a range of benefits, such as reduced admission charges to museums, cinemas, theatres and ancient sites, plus discounts on public transport. Others should declare their status upfront, as it is up to the discretion of each institution.

Electricity
Voltage	220V AC
Frequency	50Hz
Cycle	AC
Plugs	standard continental two round pins

Embassies
Australia (6, E1; ☎ 210 645 0404; D Soutsou 37, Ambelokipi)
Canada (6, D3; ☎ 210 727 3400; I Genadiou 4, Evangelismos)
Japan (6, F1; ☎ 210 723 3732; Vasilissis Sofias 64, Ambelokipi)
New Zealand (1, B2; ☎ 210 687 4701; Kifissias 268, Halandri)
South Africa (1, C1; ☎ 210 610 6645; Kifissias 60, Maroussi)
UK (6, C3; ☎ 210 727 2600; Ploutarhou 1, Kolonaki)
USA (6, E2; ☎ 210 721 2951; Vasilissis Sofias 91, Ambelokipi)

Emergencies
There's a toll-free, 24-hour emergency assistance number (☎ 112; English or French) for visitors. Other numbers include:
Ambulance	☎ 166
Fire	☎ 199
Police	☎ 100
Tourist Police	☎ 171

Fitness
SWIMMING POOLS
Unfortunately for swimmers, hotel pools are the only option in the city. Some hotels allow non-guests to use their facilities but they can be expensive.
Athens Holiday Inn (6, E3; ☎ 210 727 8000; www.hiathensgreece.com; Mihalakopoulou 50, Ilissia; ⏱ 10am-7pm, May-Oct; €15; Ⓜ Megaro Moussikis)
Divani Caravel (6,D3; ☎ 210 720 7000; www.divanicaravel.gr; Vassileos Alexandrou 2, Ilissia; ⏱ 10am-7pm; €30 weekdays, €45 weekends; Ⓜ Evangelismos)

Hilton (6, D3; ☎ 210 728 1000; Vasilissis Sofias 46, Athens; ☽ 10am-7pm; €30, weekends €35; Ⓜ Evangelismos)
Park Hotel (7, D1; ☎ 210 883 2711; www.parkhotel.gr; Alexandras 10, Areos Park; ☽ 10.30am-6.30pm; €20, including coffee or soft drink; Ⓜ Viktoria)

BEACHES
Most of the organised beaches close to Athens, set up in the '60s, have been privatised and upgraded. They have change rooms and snack bars, with some boasting tennis courts, water slides, playgrounds, beach bikes and canoes. They stay open late during heat waves. The Varkiza beach, part of the Astir resort, even has cabanas for afternoon siestas. The following are in order of distance from Athens.
Alimo (1, B3; ☎ 210 985 8650; ☽ 8am-8pm; €3)
Varkiza (2, D2; ☎ 210 894 8251; ☽ 8am-8pm; Mon-Fri €7, Sat & Sun €10)
Voula (1, B3; ☎ 210 895 1646; ☽ 7am-9pm; €3/1.50)
Vouliagmeni (2, D2 ☎ 210 9673184; ☽ 8am-8pm; €3)

Bus A2 from Panepistimiou (in front of the Academy) stops at Alimo and Voula. To get to Vouliagmeni and Varkiza, get off at Glyfada and transfer to bus 115. In summer there are express buses all the way to Varkiza.

DIVING & SNORKELLING
The accredited **Aegean Dive Centre** (4, C2; ☎ 210 894 5409; www.adc .gr; Zamanou 53, Glyfada; snorkelling shore/boat €20-25, diving €32-50) offers daily boat and shore dives, night dives, boat trips and snorkelling. There is also a special Discover Scuba course for kids (in a pool). Most dives are around Varkiza, and one to two days' notice is required.

GOLF
The 18-hole **Glyfada Golf Course** (4, B1; ☎ 210 894 6820; www.glyfada golf.gr; Konstantinos Karamanlis, Glyfada; ☽ 7.30am-dusk Tue-Sun, 1pm-dusk Mon; green fees Mon-Fri €70, Sat-Sun €82, buggy hire 9/18 holes €16/30, electric cart hire €6, club hire €20, lockers free) is the only course in town. It has a restaurant, bar, club rooms and a Pro-Shop. Call well in advance for weekend bookings.

Gay & Lesbian Travellers
Homosexuality is generally frowned upon, but there is tolerance of gays and lesbians. The local gay community is not very visible, although a significant closet culture exists. It would be wise not to be openly affectionate in public unless you are in a dedicated gay venue.

That said, Athens has a busy gay bar scene, centred mostly around Makrigianni, south of the Temple of Olympian Zeus.

INFORMATION & ORGANISATIONS
There's basic information for travellers on the Internet at: www.geo cities.com/WestHollywood/2225 /index.html or www.gaygreece.gr, or you can check out the Spartacus gay travel guide. Lesbian sites include www.lesbian.gr and http:// geocities.com/sapphida/loa/eg/.

Health
IMMUNISATIONS
No vaccinations are required for entry into Greece. A yellow fever vaccination certificate is required if you are coming from an infected area. Routine tetanus, diphtheria, polio and hepatitis A inoculations are generally recommended.

PRECAUTIONS
Health conditions in Athens are generally excellent and tap water is drinkable. The heat in summer can

be stifling, so drink plenty of water to avoid dehydration and heat exhaustion, and wear sunscreen, sensible light clothing and a hat.

Like anywhere else, practise the usual precautions when it comes to safe sex; condoms are available at pharmacies and supermarkets.

MEDICAL SERVICES

Accident and emergency treatment is available 24 hours per day at duty hospitals, which operate on a roster basis. Dial ☎ 106 for information about the nearest emergency hospital or check the listings in the daily *IHT/Kathimerini* or *Athens News*. A round-the-clock service is provided by SOS Doctors, who charge a fixed rate for hotel or home visits, but they do accept credit cards (☎ 1016).

Major hospitals include:

Agia Sofia (6, F1; ☎ 210 746 7000; Thivon & Mikras Asias, Goudi) Children's public hospital.

Athens Euroclinic (6, E1; ☎ 210 641 6600, emergencies 1011; Athanasiadou 9, Ambelokipi) Private hospital.

Evangelismos (6, C3; ☎ 210 720 1000; Ypsilandou 45-47, Kolonaki) Public hospital.

DENTAL SERVICES

If you chip a tooth or require emergency treatment it's best to ask at your hotel or contact your embassy. Minor procedures will require cash, but if you have travel insurance you will be able to claim any expenses when you get home.

PHARMACIES

Athens' pharmacists are well trained and licensed to dispense a wide range of medicines that elsewhere only doctor can prescribe. Most of the ones around Syntagma Sq have staff that speak at least some English. A monthly schedule of after-hours duty pharmacies is posted on pharmacy doors, and the *IHT/Kathimerini* publishes daily lists. The airport has the only permanent 24-hour pharmacy.

Holidays

January 1	New Year's Day
January 6	Epiphany
February/March	Ash Monday
March 25	Greek Independence Day
March/April	Good Friday
March/April	Easter Sunday
May 1	Labour Day/Spring Festival
June	Agios Pnevmatos
August 15	Feast of the Assumption of the Virgin
October 28	Ohi Day
December 25	Christmas Day
December 26	Agios Stephanos

Internet
INTERNET SERVICE PROVIDERS

The vast majority of global ISPs have dial-in nodes in Greece. It's best to download this information from their sites before you leave home. Greece's main ISP providers are Otenet, Forthnet and Hellas Online, however they usually require at least a one-month contract.

INTERNET CAFÉS

There are plenty of Internet cafés in Athens, charging average hourly rates of €3 to €6 and offering the usual range of computer services. Business centres, such as those at the airport, have great facilities but charge about double what you would pay at Internet cafés. A few monitors are set up at the airport allowing free access, but these tend to attract long queues.

Ivis Internet Services (9, E1; ☎ 210 324 3365; ivis@travelling.gr; Mitropoleos 3, Syntagma; per 15min €1; ☽ 8.30am-11.30pm)

Museum Internet Cafe (7, C2; ☎ 210
883 3418; www.museumcafe.gr;
28 Oktovriou-Patission 46; per 20min
€1.50; ☾ 9am-3am)

Plaka Internet World (8, F3; ☎ 210
331 6056; Pandrosou 29, Plaka; per
15min €1.50; ☾ 10am-11pm)

USEFUL WEBSITES
The Lonely Planet website (www
.lonelyplanet.com) offers a speedy
link to many Greek websites. Others
to try include:

Greece Now www.greece.gr
Greek Travel Pages www.gtp.gr
Ministry of Culture www.culture.gr

Lost Property
The best course of action is to call
the 24-hour tourist police number
(☎ 171) and explain where you
lost your property. They can refer
you to the appropriate department.

Metric System
The metric system is standard. Like
other Europeans, Greeks use com-
mas in decimals and points to indicate thousands. See the conversion
table below.

TEMPERATURE
°C = (°F - 32) ÷ 1.8
°F = (°C x 1.8) + 32

°C		°F
50	45	120
40	35	110
30	25	100 90
20	15	80 70
10	5	60 50
0	-5	40 30
-10	-15	20 10
-20	-25	0 -10
-30	-35	-20 -30
-40		-40

DISTANCE
1in = 2.54cm
1cm = 0.39in
1m = 3.3ft = 1.1yd
1ft = 0.3m
1km = 0.62 miles
1 mile = 1.6km

WEIGHT
1kg = 2.2lb
1lb = 0.45kg
1g = 0.04oz
1oz = 28g

VOLUME
1L = 0.26 US gallons
1 US gallon = 3.8L
1L = 0.22 imperial gallons
1 imperial gallon = 4.55L

Money
CURRENCY
Greece adopted the single EU currency, the euro (pronounced 'evro'
in Greek) on 1 January 2002. The
drachma was completely phased
out by 1 March 2002.

TRAVELLERS CHEQUES
Amex, Visa, Thomas Cook and
Euro-cheques are widely accepted
and have efficient replacement
policies but cannot be used as hard
currency. You can cash travellers
cheques in all banks, exchange
bureaus and big hotels. American
Express (☎ 210 322 3380; Ermou
7, Syntagma) charges no commis-
sion. It's open Monday to Friday,
8.30am to 4.30pm. Have your passport with you, as ID is necessary.

CREDIT CARDS
Plastic is accepted in most hotels,
retail stores, travel- and car-rental
agencies, but not in all restaurants.
Many retailers will give you better discounts if you pay cash. The
most widely accepted cards are
American Express, Diners, Master-
Card and Visa. For assistance or to
report lost or stolen cards call:

American Express
(☎ 210 324 4975-9,
☎ toll-free 00 800 44 122296)
Diners Club
(☎ 210 929 0200)
MasterCard/Eurocard
(☎ 210 950 3600, 210 929 0100)
Visa International
(☎ toll-free 00 800 11 638 0304)

ATMS
ATMs are everywhere in Athens,
including metro stations; most operate in several languages. Cirrus,
Plus and Maestro users can also
make withdrawals all over town.
Some banks around Syntagma also
have automatic foreign exchange
machines that take all major

European currencies, Australian and US dollars and Japanese yen.

CHANGING MONEY

Licensed foreign exchange bureaus can be found around Omonia and Syntagma. Shop around, but banks usually offer the most competitive rates.

Eurochange (7, C3; ☎ 210 523 4816; Omonias 10, Plateia Omonia; ☯ 8am-9pm)

Eurochange (9, E2; ☎ 210 324 3997; Filellinon 22, Plaka; ☯ 8am-9pm)

Eurochange (7, D5; ☎ 210 331 2462; Karageorgi Servias 2, Syntagma; ☯ 8am-9pm)

National Bank of Greece (7, D5; ☎ 210 334 0500; Karageorgi Servias 6, Syntagma; ☯ 8am-2.30 pm & 3.30-6.30pm Mon-Thu, 8am-2.00pm & 3.30-6.30pm Fri, 9am-3pm Sat, 9am-1pm Sun)

Newspapers & Magazines

Greeks are avid news followers as the 15 daily newspapers confirm.

The biggest selection of foreign press publications can be found at the 24-hour kiosks in Omonia and Syntagma, and in Kolonaki Sq.

The only English-language daily paper (except Sunday) is the eight-page edition of *Kathimerini* (www .kathimerini.gr), published with the *International Herald Tribune*. The weekly *Athens News* (www .athensnews.gr) carries Greek and international news and features. Both publications print movie and entertainment listings.

The bimonthly *Odyssey* magazine publishes a handy annual summer guide to Athens and Greece, while the monthly city magazine *Insider* taps into what's happening. The Greek-language weeklies *Time Out Athens* and *Athinorama* are the best source of information about events in the city, but only if you can read Greek. *Time Out* also

publishes an annual visitor's guide in English during the summer.

Opening Hours

Banking hours are Monday to Thursday, 8am to 2.30pm and Friday 8am to 2pm.

Department stores and supermarkets open Monday to Friday 8am to 8pm, Saturday 8am to 3pm. Other shops usually open Monday, Wednesday and Saturday 9am to 3pm, Tuesday, Thursday and Friday 9am to 2.30pm and 5.30pm to 8.30pm, or 5pm to 8pm in winter.

Open early morning until late, Athen's kiosks (periptera) are extremely handy. Some are even open 24 hours a day, especially in areas around Syntagma and Omonia.

Most suburban post offices open Monday to Friday, 7.30am to 2pm. In the city centre, the post office at Syntagma Square is open Monday to Friday 7.30am to 8pm, Saturday 7.30am to 2pm and Sunday 9am to 1pm, while the Central Post Office at Omonia is open 24 hours.

Photography & Video

Most major brands and types of film are available, as are black-and-white film, slide film and camera gear and repairs. Developing a roll of 36 single exposures costs about €8.

Greece uses the PAL video system, which is incompatible with the North American and Japanese NTSC and the French Secam, unless you have a multi-system machine.

Post

The mail system is quite efficient now. Post offices are easily identifiable by their yellow signs; there can still be long queues (tahidromia), but at least you take a number. Many larger post offices now have stamp vending machines and fax and courier services. The main city post offices are **Athens Central Post**

Office (7, C3; Eolou 100, Omonia), and one at **Syntagma Sq** (7, D5).

POSTAL RATES
Postcards and airmail letters to EU destinations cost €0.65/€1 for up to 20/50g. Other destinations cost €0.60/€1.15 for up to 20/50g. Post within the EU takes seven to eight days, or nine to 11 days to the USA, Australia and New Zealand. Some tourist shops also sell stamps, but with a 10% surcharge. Express mail costs an extra €2 and should ensure delivery in three days within the EU. Valuables should be sent by registered post, which costs an extra €2.20.

Radio
Athens has more than 20 radio stations, and between they play everything from hip-hop to Greek folk music.

ERA 1 Pop and rock, 91.6FM

Cosmos Pop and rock, 93.6FM

ERA 3 Classical music, 107.7FM

Galaxy CNN news briefs and foreign pop, 92.0FM

Flash Daily English news bulletins at 9am, 3pm and 8pm, 96.0FM

Village Latest music, 88.2FM

Radio Gold Retro, 105 FM

Kiss Rock and techno, 92.9FM

Nitro Alternative rock, 108.2FM

Ciao Greek pop, 104.2FM

Melodia Greek nostalgia, 99.3FM

BBC World Service Daily news bulletins at 9am, 10pm and midnight on weekdays, 7am, 9am, 2pm and 4pm on weekends. Weeknights, continuous broadcast between 2am and 7am, 88.7 FM.

Telephone
There are public phones all over Athens. The I (information) button provides user instructions in English. All booths take phonecards, giving you a specific number of units depending on the cost of the card. Local calls cost one unit per minute.

PHONECARDS
All kiosks, corner shops and tourist shops sell phonecards (€3/6.50/20) allowing domestic and international calls.

Lonely Planet's eKno Communication Card provides competitive rates for international calls (although you should try to avoid using it for local calls), messaging services and free email for travellers.

Visit the eKno website at www .ekno.lonelyplanet.com for details on joining and accessing this handy service.

MOBILE PHONES
Greece uses the same GSM system as most EU countries, Asia and Australia. Before you go, check that your service provider offers international roaming. Greece's main mobile phone service providers are TeleStet, CosmOTE and Vodafone.

North America and Japan use a cellular phone system that is incompatible with Europe. Phones can be rented from some hotels as well as **Euroline** (☎ 210 985 9990) and **Rent-a-phone** (☎ 210 931 9951).

COUNTRY & CITY CODES
Greece	☎ 30
Athens	☎ 210

USEFUL PHONE NUMBERS
Domestic Operator	☎ 151, 152
Duty Hospitals/Pharmacies	☎ 1434
First Aid Centre	☎ 168
International Directory	☎ 161
International Operator	☎ 161
Local Directory Inquiries	☎ 131
Reverse-Charge (collect)	☎ 161
SOS Doctors	☎ 1016
Time	☎ 141
Tourist Police	☎ 171
Weather	☎ 1448

TV

Greece has several private TV channels but most are very ordinary. Channel surfing might get you a movie in English, MAD TV music videos or some old episodes of your favourite US soaps. The state-run ET 1, ET 3 and NET have quality programmes, documentaries and news in Greek. Cable TV is available but not widespread.

Time

Athens is two hours ahead of GMT, one hour ahead of Central European Time and seven hours ahead of US Eastern Standard Time. Daylight-savings is in effect from the last Sunday in March to the last Sunday in October.

Tipping

Tipping is customary but not compulsory. In restaurants, the service charge is included in the bill, but most people still leave a small tip or at least round off the bill. This applies to taxis as well – a small tip for good service is much appreciated.

Toilets

Public toilets are rare in Athens, so head to fast food places like McDonald's (although plans were afoot to install portable toilets all over the city for the Olympics). If you really get stuck, most restaurants will allow you to use their restrooms if you ask politely.

Don't forget that those little bins in all toilets are for paper waste, so never flush toilet paper down the toilet. It might seem a little third-world and quirky, but it helps avoid clogging the system.

Tourist Information

Information on Athens is available from the **Greek National Tourism Organisation** (GNTO; www.gnto.gr), referred to as EOT in Greek.

The GNTO has multilingual staff and information on all aspects of the city, including various maps, travel brochures, public transport and ferry timetables, and assistance with hotel bookings. Unfortunately, the central office moved along with the GNTO headquarters to new premises in Ambelokipi in early 2003, leaving the city centre with no tourist information office or booth. Plans to remedy this extraordinary oversight, presumably in time for the Olympics, are in motion.

The Tourist Police have a 24-hour tourist information hotline on ☎ 171.

Eleftherios Venizelos Airport Arrivals Terminal (2, D2; ☎ 210 353 0445-7; ☾ 8am-10pm)

EOT Information (6, E1; ☎ 210 870 7000; Tsoha 7, Ambelokipi; ☾ Mon-Fri 9am-4.30pm)

Lonely Planet offers digital information about Athens for those with mobile phones and other gadgets. Check out the latest offerings at www.lonelyplanet.com/mobile.

Women Travellers

Greek men once had a notorious reputation for pestering women, especially foreigners, but the practice (more of a nuisance than an actual threat) is far less prevalent now. Taxi drivers are usually respectful, if grumpy. However, it is always wise to avoid walking in deserted parts of the city and parks at night (especially around Omonia and Areos Park) and to use common sense.

Items for personal and sanitary hygiene are widely available in supermarkets and pharmacies. You can buy contraceptives over the counter.

LANGUAGE

The official language is Greek, but many people, particularly younger folk, speak English.

Probably the oldest European language, Greek has an oral tradition dating back some 4000 years and a written tradition of about 3000 years. Modern Greek developed from a number of regional dialects, mainly from the south. Greek has its own distinctive 24-letter alphabet, from which the Cyrillic alphabet was derived. Transliterations into the Roman alphabet are used in this guide; note that the letter combination dh is pronounced as the 'th' in 'them'.

BASICS

Hello.	*yasas*
	yasu (informal)
Goodbye.	*andio*
Good morning.	*kalimera*
Good afternoon.	*herete*
Good evening.	*kalispera*
Please.	*parakalo*
Thank you.	*efharisto*
Yes.	*ne*
No.	*ohi*
Sorry. (excuse me, forgive me)	*sighnomi*
How are you?	*ti kanete?*
	ti kanis? (informal)
I'm well, thanks.	*kala efharisto*
Do you speak English?	*milate anglika?*
I understand.	*katalaveno*
I don't understand.	*dhen katalaveno*
Where is ...?	*pou ine ...?*
How much?	*poso kani?*
When?	*pote?*

GETTING AROUND

What time does the ... leave/arrive?	*ti ora fevyi/ftani to ...?*
boat	*karavi*
train	*treno*
I'd like a return ticket.	*tha ithela isitirio me epistrofi*
metro station	*metro stathmos*
Where is ...?	*pou ine ...?*

Is it far?	*ine makria?*
How do I get to ...?	*pos tha pao sto/sti ...?*

ACCOMMODATION

I'd like a ...	*thelo ena ...*
single	*mono*
double	*dhiplo*
room with	*dhomatio*
bathroom	*me banio*

AROUND TOWN

I'm looking for (the) ...	*psahno ya ...*
bank	*tin trapeza*
beach	*tin paralia*
kiosk	*to periptero*
market	*tin aghora*
museum	*to musio*
ruins	*ta arhaia*

TIME, DAYS &NUMBERS

What time is it?	*ti ora ine?*
It's ...	*ine ...*
today	*simera*
tonight	*apopse*
now	*tora*
yesterday	*hthes*
tomorrow	*avrio*

Sunday	*kyriaki*
Monday	*dheftera*
Tuesday	*triti*
Wednesday	*tetarti*
Thursday	*pempti*
Friday	*paraskevi*
Saturday	*savato*

0	*midhen*
1	*ena*
2	*dhio*
3	*tria*
4	*tesera*
5	*pende*
6	*exi*
7	*epta*
8	*ohto*
9	*enea*
10	*dheka*
100	*ekato*
1000	*hilia*

Index

See also separate indexes for Eating (p125), Sleeping (p126), Shopping (p126) and Sights Index with map references (p127).

EATING

SLEEPING

SHOPPING

Sights Index

FEATURES

- Eating
- Entertainment, Drinking, Cafe
- Highlights
- Shopping
- Sights/Activities
- Sleeping
- Olympic Site

ROUTES

- Tollway
- Freeway
- Primary Road
- Secondary Road
- Tertiary Road
- Lane
- Under Construction
- One-Way Street
- Unsealed Road
- Mall/Steps
- Tunnel
- Walking Path
- Track
- Walking Tour

BOUNDARIES

- State, Provincial
- Regional, Suburb
- Ancient Wall

TRANSPORT

- Airport, Airfield
- Bus Route
- Cable-Car, Funicular
- Cycling, Bicycle Path
- Ferry
- General Transport
- Metro
- Monorail
- Rail
- Taxi Rank
- Trail Head
- Tram

AREAS

- Beach, Desert
- Building
- Land
- Mall
- Other Area
- Park/Cemetary
- Sports
- Urban

HYDROGRAPHY

- River, Creek
- Intermittent River
- Canal
- Swamp
- Water

SYMBOLS

- Bank, ATM
- Buddhist
- Castle, Fortress
- Christian
- Diving, Snorkeling
- Embassy, Consulate
- Hospital, Clinic
- Information
- Internet Access
- Islamic
- Jewish
- Lighthouse
- Lookout
- Monument
- Mountain, Volcano
- National Park
- Parking Area
- Petrol Station
- Picnic Area
- Point of Interest
- Police Station
- Post Office
- Ruin
- Telephone
- Toilets
- Zoo, Bird Sanctuary
- Waterfall

24/7 travel advice
www.lonelyplanet.com